Praise for *Is Your Job Making You Ill?*

'Dr Ellie Cannon has produced an incredibly helpful guide to dealing with ill health at work. It's not just for those who are unwell but for the people around them too. I have spoken to many staff in HR about stress and mental health-related issues at work and I believe this book is a must-read for them as well. Mental illness has become a rapidly increasing cause for concern within the workplace and very few people know how to navigate this. Dr Ellie's book gives comprehensive advice and practical words of wisdom from her years of experience that will be extremely reassuring to anyone who is struggling'

Jonny Benjamin, MBE, mental health campaigner, writer, filmmaker and public speaker

'*Is Your Job Making You Ill* contains good, sound advice from Dr Ellie Cannon. It is well worth reading for anyone who is struggling at work and needs a framework for thinking differently about it'

Karen Mattison, MBE, joint CEO Timewise

DR ELLIE
CANNON

Is Your Job Making You Ill?

piatkus

PIATKUS

First published in Great Britain in 2018 by Piatkus

1 3 5 7 9 10 8 6 4 2

A CIP catalogue record for this book
is available from the British Library.

ISBN 978-0-349-41674-8

Typeset in Stone Serif by M Rules
Printed and bound in Great Britain by
Clays Ltd, St Ives plc

ests

An Hachette UK Company
www.hachette.co.uk

www.improvementzone.co.uk

Dr Ellie Cannon is the current face of NHS general practice. Ellie read medicine at Cambridge University and then completed her clinical training at the Royal Free Hospital, London before embarking on a career in General Practice. A young, vivacious, approachable doctor, she is best known for her weekly health column in the *Mail on Sunday* and *Mailonline*. She is also a frequent contributor to *Netdoctor*, the resident GP columnist for *Best* Magazine and is widely quoted across all media on health matters. As well as being the on-screen GP for Sky News *Sunrise* and the regular doctor on LBC's *Health Hour,* she was one of the key medical experts on Channel 4's *Health Freaks* and *Doctor in Your House.* Recently she even channelled her inner-geek, appearing on the TV Doctors team on *Celebrity Eggheads. Is Your Job Making You Ill?* is her second book.

For Adam

Contents

Introduction

We all have a moan about going to work. We groan about getting on that bus in the rush hour, complain about Monday morning blues and long for it to be the weekend again.

Work takes up the majority of our week – and sometimes the majority of our socialising – and for all of us it provides that vital aspect of day-to-day life, income. Work, employment, is a defining and significant aspect of any adult's life, taking up sizeable chunks of time, focus and energy. So a gripe here and there throughout our working lives is understandable and expected; we all moan about the boss or laugh at the office stereotypes, and joke about the pain of Monday mornings and the thrill of that Friday feeling.

But for many people now in the UK, work has ceased to be simply a source of grumbles or a joke, and the negative effects from work have become far more detrimental to wellbeing than just Sunday-night blues. For them their job has started to make them mentally or physically unwell.

This may seem unfathomable to some – it can be hard to empathise if your working life is content. But after a decade in general practice in the NHS I have seen just how ubiquitous and extensive work-related ill health is. Seeing a patient who has become either physically or mentally ill through a work-related cause has become a normal, standard consultation for me, accounting for at least one or two patients that I see a week.

At the start of my career I would have found it pretty hard to identify work-related ill health as a significant problem. I certainly didn't have any understanding of just how pervasive the issue is. As a newly qualified GP I expected to see cancer and depression and chicken pox, of course. But I never would have added work-related illness to that sad bunch. I had no idea just how substantial the problem was.

I remember very clearly, as a GP registrar, dealing with my first case of work stress: a man who had been (wrongly) accused of using a company car inappropriately, and who was struggling to sleep at nights as he coped with the terms of his suspension and the formal disciplinary proceedings. It was a defining moment for me as a GP: seeing the way that a job could have such an impact on a person's health. This is when I realised just how strong the connection is between the physical, mental and social aspects of our lives. My senior colleagues were less shaken, less interested in what to them was commonplace. But I was sure this was an unusual situation, a rare consultation and probably not to be repeated often.

I was categorically wrong and quite simply naïve about that! As the months and years of my general practice career went by I began to see what my older colleagues already understood: what a substantial and significant problem work-related ill health is, and how it is, sadly, pretty common. And after over ten years working as a GP, there is enough of a problem to compel me to write this book to help others suffering in the same way.

I want to share the insights and experiences I have explored with my patients: what has worked, what hasn't, and why anyone can find themselves affected. Work-related ill health can affect a huge range of workers, from the highest-earning CEOs to the those at the bottom of the office heap. It can happen to anyone and it's nothing to be ashamed of.

This book is all about how to survive and thrive when it happens to you.

On a totally normal Thursday in clinic one February, out of forty patients I saw or spoke to, three discussed with me how their job was making them ill. Given this was an ordinary day, in a very typical general practice, this illustrates just how prevalent the issue is. When you think that in a typical day I would see only three or four cases of other conditions you would consider to be very commonplace, such as asthma or diabetes, this is clearly very significant.

The first patient worked in retail. She was a bubbly, bright, gregarious lady working for a large retail chain to whom she felt very loyal, having worked her way up the ladder over seven years. She was simply on the phone for a review of her antidepressant medication. I was curious to know when she had started taking them and she told me it had been a couple of years. The manager at work, she didn't hesitate to tell me, bullied everyone, yet she was quite clear it was a fantastic job for her, a great opportunity and not something to give up. The bullying had led her to a change in mood a couple of years earlier and, in the end, she and her previous GP agreed on trying medication, which had been successful.

I was really fascinated by her approach to the issue, and this is what can happen in the workplace to many people, not just her: you take it on the chin, deal with it and carry on. She needed the job – and very much enjoyed it, despite the manager – so she felt she had to be pragmatic about making her life work, and about managing her health. She had a strict regime of Pilates twice a week, cycling to work once a week, and eating healthily. She ensured that while work was a source of illness for her, she could forge a feasible solution without giving up her job.

The second case I saw was a young man with back pain. Doctors tend not to see ongoing back pain in young adults, so when we do it is always a reason to think a bit more and investigate. In this case we were initiating a referral to a specialist in case it was a type of juvenile-onset arthritis, a diagnosis which is very important to pick up early. This man had worked since leaving school, and had an incredibly strong work ethic. (I am keen to point this out here as there is sometimes a misconception that work-related illness, particularly in younger workers, could just be malingering or an excuse. I do not believe that.)

I was worried even at the outset of his pain that this patient's job in a call centre, sitting at a desk for hours at a stretch, was worsening his pain. There were no timed breaks, and with the phone constantly ringing there could be hours in a row with no standing up and no walking around – a curse for anyone with any back pain. It is generally recommended for back pain that you keep moving, with gentle stretching to stop you seizing up. So as part of my initial management when I'd seen the man a month earlier, I had given him a 'fit note': a note from a doctor saying that the person is fit to work, but only with certain conditions in place. In this case I had suggested simply that he needed regular movement breaks to stop him stiffening up. He just needed to walk around the office, or even make calls standing rather than sitting. But the young man's manager, while at first accepting the conditions of the fit note, didn't ensure they were put in place in any formal way, and then started to question the need for these special arrangements when no one else at the call centre had them.

After a week or so, my patient was back sitting at his desk for hours again. He was fearful of getting up too often and being reprimanded, and losing a job he really needed. So with no time or space to recover (which we had tried to foster without sick leave, because he didn't want to be off sick), and without the movement breaks he needed, his back pain deteriorated. In clinic that day I had to issue a sick note: sitting all day, combined with a boss who refused to accommodate my medical advice, was worsening his illness and not allowing him the recovery he needed. With his job making him ill, I had no choice but to recommend he temporarily stop to see if we could improve his health. He was terribly disappointed.

'I actually thought I was having a heart attack' was how the third patient of the day described the way he felt when he went back into the office to face a colleague who had tormented co-workers for over five years. My patient had started that job a couple of years earlier, wide-eyed and keen to work in a management role within a field that had always been his passion. Over the previous two years his morale, self-esteem and enjoyment of life had been quashed by this colleague who had a long history of manipulation and bullying that had never been brought to task. He told me his workmates were taking daily medication to cope with the atmosphere and this colleague's attitude, and one was seeking help for alcoholism. My patient was shocked to find himself experiencing difficulty breathing, pains all over his body and his heart racing one Sunday, when he was due to go back into the office after some annual leave. We discussed this as a possible panic attack. In nine years of being my patient he had never once sought medical help for anxiety or panic, despite going through major traumatic life events, and yet his work managed to tip him over that line. He breathed a sigh of relief to hear it could be a panic attack and this only affirmed the decision he had made while on his annual leave to resign, as – luckily – he had found another job. He did

have a month-long notice period to work out, and we discussed whether he would need a beta-blocker prescription to
cope with any further panic attacks. He declined.

It is likely you see your own symptoms or work situations
reflected in these cases. Whether familiar or not, I hope these
examples illustrate for you just how wide-ranging job-related
illness can be, and how different the symptoms and the sufferers can be. It comes in many different forms and is caused
by a whole host of factors, but whatever your own individual
scenario, your work-related illness needs to be tackled and
treated like any other health issue.

My experience as an inner-city GP since 2006 may have
opened my eyes to the issue of work-related ill health, but the
statistics speak for themselves.

Figures from the Labour Force Survey from 2015/16 estimate
that the number of cases of work-related stress, depression or
anxiety was 488,000 in the UK. For every 100,000 people
going to work, this means 1,510 will be affected by these illnesses. This explains how a GP working a normal week in
surgery could see at least one or two cases a week, whether
those cases are newly affected patients or those for whom this
is an ongoing issue. For the past decade the number of new
cases of these work-related illnesses has remained broadly the
same; there is clearly a need for awareness and change to bring
about any improvement in these numbers.

Although the figures are astounding, I really believe they
could be an underestimate, as work-related ill health can
easily go unreported. Many sufferers may not complain or
acknowledge the issue due to embarrassment, so would not
be included in official figures. Others may not be aware that
work could be a cause of their ill health, or may not choose
to discuss it with a doctor or healthcare professional, so again
would not be part of any official statistics. It is not uncommon

for a patient to ask me not to write the words 'work' or 'job' in their records, or on a sick note, leading me to believe there is a sizeable amount of underreporting – and therefore under-acknowledgement – of jobs as a source of illness. Additionally, these official figures will only include the three diagnoses cited: stress, depression and anxiety. While these are the most significant, there are many more illnesses, both physical and psychological, that will bump up those numbers.

Of course, it is not only the individual who suffers as a result of these work-related illnesses. Work-related stress, depression and anxiety accounted for *11.7 million* lost working days in the UK in 2015/16, with the average sufferer taking over 23 days off work sick. Undoubtedly this has a huge impact on the economy at every level.

Why I Wrote This Book

I have seen that work-related ill health can happen to any one, no matter who they are or what they do. It doesn't seem to discriminate, although according to the Labour Force Survey the problem is certainly more prevalent in those within public-sector industries such as education, healthcare, public administration and the military. You are more likely to suffer from stress within certain jobs; teaching, healthcare, business, media and public service show higher rates of stress when compared to other occupations. I know that it was one September a few years ago, after seeing a deluge of teachers with work-related illness, that the enormity of the issue was cemented in my mind.

Yet, when you are in this situation yourself it can be very difficult to know where to turn, who to speak to or where to find good quality help and bona fide advice. Patients often feel there is a lack of focused help or points of reference to support them. It will usually take quite a few consultations within a GP clinic to unpick the issue and acknowledge the problems, and then even more to start formulating and adopting a plan of action, therapy and recovery. And many people, of course, don't want to ask anyone for help – not even a doctor – for fear of judgement, stigma or embarrassment.

So my aim was to feature all the ideas, objectives and solutions from those consultations in a single book, covering all the facets that work-related ill health touches. Essentially, this book is a self-help guide to stopping your job making you ill. Clearly there is a need among those affected for such help in a single reference manual, mined from the experience of others who have been in the same situation and managed a recovery.

There is also another tricky conundrum to overcome with job-related illness that I really hope to solve with this book. Often patients tell me that because they are so busy, anxious or stressed out with the work that is the cause of their woe in the first place, it can be unthinkable to consider making the time to even contemplate sorting it out. With work taking up so much of our lives – and so much of our thoughts when it is making us ill – it can be impossible to get any clarity on the situation. Relaxation time becomes so precious, the last thing you want to be thinking about is your job and the way it is making you feel. Thoughts and worries can become a whirlwind, perpetuating and worsening the issue and creating a very tricky vicious cycle.

To solve the problem you really need to make the time and the headspace to think about it and address it, which can be very challenging. I see this book as a starting point and a first step for those thoughts, as well as a way to make the headspace and time (even just a few minutes) to think about what could be going on. The clarity you need to start the process comes on these pages.

How to Use This Book

The fundamental aim of this book is to calm, empower and advise you if you are suffering work-related ill health. Consulting it may be your first step if you haven't disclosed to anybody what you are going through. Or it may provide additional guidance and support on top of help you are receiving already.

There is certainly no one-size-fits-all approach to treating job-related ill health, and I would also challenge anyone who says there is a right way to deal with it or a wrong way. In addition, the spectrum of individuals affected, as well as the range of illnesses and job environments, of course dictates that there can't be a quick, one-stop solution. For some patients I see, the toughest hurdle they face is recognising or admitting their job is the problem; I have had patients only acknowledge this years later, or only after they have left the job and could finally grasp just how unwell they had become. For other patients, it has been finding a way out that proves the most challenging, or continuing in a job you love that seems to hate you. So there are many ideas, suggestions and plans included in this book as to what can and may help. Most likely you will cherry-pick your own solutions from my suggestions to forge the right path for your individual situation.

The first step though, quite simply, has to be to accept, acknowledge and affirm the issue. You cannot find a solution if you don't see there is a problem.

To help you identify the issues you are dealing with, in the first three chapters I examine the causes of job-related illness and describe the most common illnesses and symptoms people experience. I show you how to acknowledge your own work-related ill health as a problem, as well as to diagnose it.

No recovery can even begin until you accept this

fundamental start. For many people, this could be the trickiest part, and embracing the ideas and plan in Chapter 4,
where we start the process of dealing with the problem, can
be emotionally hard. This may be the first time in your life
you are ill, the first time you think a mental health problem
could be affecting you, or it may simply be a massive dent
to your pride and a great disappointment. These are very
common feelings and they can be pretty distressing and
difficult to deal with. So as you begin this book, focus on
the knowledge that only with acceptance and affirmation at
the outset can you start to build your recovery and wellness,
and change your working life. Acceptance will help you to
focus on positive self-change and forge a plan that will be
sustainable.

When facing any illness, whether physical or psychological, structuring a recovery is key. Usually this is done for you
by healthcare professionals dictating what to do and the
therapeutic measures to try. With work-related illnesses, however, the recovery has to be far more patient-driven, focusing
on and tailored to your individual working life, career ladder
and multiple other factors that need addressing. By necessity,
a large part of your recovery will be self-directed, and the
second half of the book will guide you through that process,
starting from Chapter 5. Illness makes anyone feel powerless
and out of control, but I would hope that this book gives
back a level of control to you as an individual, an employee
and a patient.

I am a huge believer that small changes and small ideas
are as important as the big, headline ones. This is what psychologists term 'micro-actions' and these are well known to
effect change. That is why the plan of how to help yourself
in Chapter 6 covers what may seem at first like trivial issues:
your diet, your exercise levels, your journey to work. It can
be hard to fathom how reducing your caffeine intake can

possibly achieve anything when you are faced with a gargantuan, all-consuming issue such as the boss from hell, but I urge you to consider these micro-actions as an important part of the recovery process.

Because you will most likely, despite your illness, have the ability and resources within you to adopt small, 'trivial' changes, these are the most likely to succeed at the beginning of your recovery. And any success, particularly when you are coming from the point of weakness that illness can be, is a positive first step. The momentum of your first positive change, however small, allows you to build on it and be more confident about making bigger changes. And that positivity will diffuse into the other, more significant aspects of the problem that you need to try to adapt or deal with. So do not underestimate the power of the micro-action, however trivial it may seem.

I have spent many years in general practice seeing a plethora of different patients through work-related illness, and exploring what can and what does work. Thankfully, the vast majority come out the other side healthier, happier and recovered.

Your recovery starts now.

CHAPTER 1

•

What Causes
Work-related Ill Health?

In the Western world we very much define ourselves by the work we do. We often use our jobs as an introduction and a window into our lives when we meet someone: we live in a culture where the job is very much the quantifiable measure of us. It defines the clothes we wear, the holidays we take, where we live and how our kids paint us. So admitting it has all gone wrong, of course, is traumatic. When all around there seem to be people just like you who are working and getting on well with their jobs, it is natural to question how your own could possibly be affecting you so negatively.

Around half a million workers in the UK are ill as a result of their job, and there are many factors at play in why this happens. Employment, a job and a career, should be a very positive influence on someone's life, health and happiness. Unfortunately, various circumstances can arise that can turn your job into a source of illness.

Clearly, with so many people affected in so many different areas of employment, there will not be one unique factor causing job-related ill health. In fact, studies show that there are many elements within a workplace that contribute or exacerbate work-related ill health. In my experience of dealing with these issues with patients, there is often more than one problem.

It is so important for you to understand the factors that can cause work-related ill health. This has to be the first step. To build a recovery and a solution, you have to appreciate what has 'gone wrong'. As you will see, these may not be elements that you can fix. However, understanding how your job-related illness has arisen will allow you to accept the problem, build a realistic solution and move on.

The UK's Office of National Statistics' Labour Force Survey points to 'workload' as the biggest cause of psychological and psychosomatic illness from work, including stress, anxiety and depression. Specifically, 'workload' refers to tight deadlines, too much work or too much pressure and responsibility on you as an employee. Other analyses add that interpersonal relationships at work, as well as the amount of support available, are huge factors influencing wellness at work.

Anecdotally from my years in practice, I would cite relationships and team issues as being the most common causes of work-related illness I come across. From bullying bosses to toxic colleagues, there have been times in clinic when I have simply been amazed at how grown adults in responsible, highly paid jobs can behave. (In fairness, I must also add that I have often been delighted at how supportive, empathetic and helpful employers and managers can be.) A job is very much made or broken by the people around you, and the health consequences from that can be dramatic.

Personality type and personal circumstances will also interact with the factors at work and influence how affected an individual is by their difficult work circumstances: we saw this with my patient working in retail who learnt to cope with her horrible boss through the strategies she implemented outside work. Individual resilience, background, health and personal factors will allow you to be more susceptible or stronger at different times in your life. Aspects of your job that may feel manageable most of the time, when life is generally good, can become a source of illness if you are going through a personal issue such as bereavement or divorce, which can knock your resilience and ability to cope and bring about illness.

Let's look at the most common negative situations that are proven to contribute to work-related ill health. The idea of working through these in turn is to offer you some potential answers as to the source of your own issue: there certainly could be more than one that feels familiar to your own situation. Spelling them out for you at this stage allows you to understand the pathway that led to your illness, which in turn allows you to forge the pathway to your recovery.

Workload

As we have seen, statistics looking at work-related ill health in the UK cite 'workload' as the biggest cause of stress, anxiety and depression. Tight deadlines, too much pressure and responsibility, and simply too much work have been identified as the main contributors that can detrimentally affect the health of employees.

Anyone going to work should be able to feel they can cope with their job: not that it is easy and unfulfilling, but that they have both the personal and external resources to cope, enjoy and succeed. That comes from being in an appropriate role and having suitable amounts of work, as well as having good supervision and managerial support. In environments where there is a continuous feeling of 'only just coping' and 'firefighting' all the time, there tend to be high rates of work-related ill health caused by feeling under pressure and on edge all the time. Feeling as if you are struggling all the time will adversely affect your self-esteem, self-worth, job satisfaction and mood. Of course, many of us go through unusually busy periods at work, and a week or so of this is fine, but when this is the constant state of play long term it is easy to see how it leads to ill health.

Having an inappropriate workload causes illness in many ways:

- Constantly being under pressure and overly busy is physically and mentally exhausting, and over time builds up levels of fatigue and burnout. Fatigue impacts on sleep patterns, mood and physical health as well as your relationships.

- The lifestyle that goes with overwork is detrimental to health. Tight deadlines and pressure encourage workers to skip breaks, work late, work into the weekend and eat on the run, preventing them from doing things that can be protective of good health. It is in exactly these situations that you need to foster good behaviours outside work to protect your health – but paradoxically, of course, after a day of being overworked it is very hard to find the motivation to exercise, make a healthy meal or engage in positive relaxation. You are far more likely to flop on the sofa and fall asleep.

- Another scenario I hear often from patients is that they have gone home after work and cannot stop thinking about work. Their mind and heart are racing, worrying about the next day, and they are unable to fall asleep. This leads to a vicious cycle of overworking and underrelaxing that very quickly fuels a poor health situation. While our minds and bodies can cope with this in the short term, for example getting to the end of a big deadline or contract (I see this a lot in accountants as the tax year-end approaches), this type of work pattern is unsustainable in the long term.

- Mentally there is little satisfaction in a job where the demands placed on you do not match your capabilities and resources. This leads to an overriding negative emotional impact from work, with feelings of guilt and poor self-esteem. Humans by nature want to succeed at their tasks, and need the fulfilment and satisfaction that comes from that. Imagine that joyful feeling when you have finished your day's to-do list, everything has gone well and you treat yourself to a coffee. If your daily work is characterised by the opposite of that, never feeling you have succeeded and it is always impossible to achieve your goals, your mental health will suffer very quickly.

Workload issues may stem from the organisational structure of the workplace, or because an individual has not been trained properly, or has been given the wrong level of responsibility. It is not uncommon for me to see this in practice, where someone has been promoted to managerial level too quickly. While it is attractive and exciting at the outset to be promoted, it can result in a situation for the individual where they are overburdened and working above their skill set, which in the long term can be unhealthy. Statistics show that this is most prevalent in public-sector industries such as education, health and social care.

Being expected to do more than you are capable of or more than is possible within strict time limits, particularly with limited resources, is often going to lead to a build-up of daily stress. That recurrent pressure, week on week, pre-cipitates ill health, whether classic stress symptoms such as irritability and fatigue, or other mental or physical conditions described in the next two chapters.

Relationships

Your team and the interpersonal relationships you have at work are vital to enjoying your job. But the effects of these social interactions go a lot further than that.

In data looking at work-related ill health, it is clear that colleagues, teams, relationships and socialising within work all have a significant role in causing job stress and other mental health problems. Essentially, the statistics show that the people you work with can really make a job; indeed, ask anyone who has a good team around them at work, and they will confirm this is the case. Conversely, when relationships go wrong in the workplace, there can be significant fallout. Relationships are the second-biggest cause of work-related ill health, after workload issues, and this is certainly something I have witnessed in general practice over the years. Bullying bosses, toxic colleagues, despotic line managers and even office affairs that have gone wrong leave patients sitting in front of me coping with the health consequences. This happens in all sorts of workplace environments – the resource-starved public sector, the high-octane, high-pressure world of big business, and anywhere people are thrown together and expected to work effectively as a team despite clashing personalities.

Having strong relationships with family and friends and supportive peers is good for emotional health and well-being, and even improves our physical health. Numerous medical studies looking at diseases such as heart disease and dementia show that social interaction, support and relation- ships are protective against certain illnesses. Conversely, being surrounded by people where there is conflict, poor relationships and confrontation will cause ill health, par- ticularly in psychological terms. In our personal life we can walk away from bad relationships, choose who we spend time with regularly and reduce the time we spend with those who do not make us feel our best. That luxury is not available at work, and it can lead to feelings of losing con- trol, anxiety and stress.

We expect to make friends and build good relationships at work because inherently we are sociable animals, and often we spend the majority of our waking hours with people at work. But a work environment is competitive – perhaps even cut-throat – and that natural drive to survive and thrive above others can conflict with our biological desire to be sociable. It is easy to see how relationships can therefore go wrong and office bullies are created.

I have come across so many instances of this, resulting in everything from trivial, isolated incidents to full-blown grievance procedures and even job loss. I was once left open- mouthed by a patient in tears who told me how much she loved her job but her colleague had turned on her, resulting in an occasion where the colleague actually locked her in the office. It was so unfathomable I think I made her repeat what had happened at least twice: I couldn't quite believe I was listening to a situation involving adults, rather than children in a playground. This case was particularly sad as my patient had always found work a solace from a difficult home life and genuinely didn't want it to 'go wrong'.

Your health can be affected not only by tricky person- alities but equally when there is a lack of support, a lack of supervision and a lack of empathy from superiors and colleagues. The line managers who don't accept a perfectly legitimate sick note or fit note and place unnecessary demands on people trying to work despite ill health; bosses who move case loads around to burden junior colleagues so that it appears they can't manage. (Twice this has happened to pregnant patients of mine, putting huge strain on women who were in fact coping incredibly well with pregnancy and a normal workload.) A work environment needs to be such that teamwork and communication is fostered, conversations are easily sought and relationships are easily built. Having a line manager or supervisor who is inaccessible or unsupportive contributes to stress and anxieties from work, and allows trivial situations to build up and escalate, worsening the health problems that ensue.

No one should go to work and be bullied or targeted unfairly, but this does happen and it will undoubtedly have health consequences. This can be to do with difficult temperaments and clashes of personalities, but may also be a result of a work environment where work patterns or set up (such as shift work or office structure) do not enable people to build other protective supportive connections with colleagues. Simply having a coffee break with colleagues for 15 minutes can be enough. If a work timetable is such that your breaks are always taken in isolation, or there is no time or space in a work day for that social contact, it is not good for your mental health. Bullying, of course, will affect anyone's health, but it is less likely to if you have other supportive relationships in the workplace.

Poor Work–Life Balance

Work–life balance seems to be what everyone is seeking, but it is hard to achieve the perfect formula. For many of us it can get a little out of kilter, swinging one way and then the other during busy and quiet periods, but most of the time feeling we have got it just about right. When it goes very wrong though, and work takes over those critical rest and leisure hours, it can have a detrimental effect on health.

To be well both psychologically and physically, people need time for rest, pleasure and leisure outside their work and chores. A poor work–life balance, where work takes up too many hours and therefore rules out these protective aspects of our lives, often leads to illness, stress and burnout. This is a common scenario, particularly in those who confuse hard work with overwork and think that productivity can only come from putting in long hours and never switching off. Achieving a healthy work–life balance can be particularly difficult for people who are freelance or self-employed, where the line between work and downtime is blurred – especially if home is also your workplace.

There is no magic formula for a good work–life balance, but no matter what our working circumstances, we all need to feel rested, well-slept and relaxed to continue to work effectively over the long term. Essentially, not having the right work–life balance allows no time to do the things that keep us healthy: spending time with friends, relaxing, eating well, exercising and nurturing your relationships. Not forgetting the all-important and restorative sleep.

Physical and mental exhaustion through overworking and underresting makes you vulnerable to ill health. Having time in a normal schedule to take care of yourself, nurture relationships and recuperate allows you to foster resilience – strong mental and physical health. It gives you the capacity to cope with stress at work, challenges and busy-ness. We all need that time to recuperate, so when that balance goes awry we suffer the health costs. It is easy to understand how too much work and too little relaxation can lead to stress, anxiety and depression. But equally, as we will see in Chapter 3, it can also lead to physical illnesses, including recurrent infections and high blood pressure.

Probably the most dramatic of all cases of work-related ill health I have seen in practice was in a very high-flying City accountant. There can be a culture within some firms of very late-night working to finish client work, followed by a taxi home in the early hours to get fresh clothes and then back to work for the next 18-hour day. It's probably possible to cope with this on the odd occasion, but sadly this woman had been subjected to this regime for many nights in a row. I saw her in clinic when this precipitated psychosis: this is a mental health condition where your thoughts and emotions are no longer related to reality. In this case, as a result of her unhealthy work pattern, she had started to have delusions that both her partner and work colleagues were conspiring against her to fail at work. This may seem an extreme example, but it can be where an unaddressed work–life balance problem is heading.

The balance between work and leisure has been profoundly rocked in the last two decades by one huge change: connectivity. The online world and smartphones have allowed us to stay connected to work far longer than we need to or should do, meaning we – inadvertently or purposely – take our work home with us on our phones. There is an expectation within our work culture now of longer and longer hours, and a damaging overuse of digital devices has permeated into precious home and family time allowing work emails, and the stress that goes with them, to intrude on family meals, exercise, nights out and even sleep. For some this has allowed freedom: the ability to work from home to ease a commute or childcare commitments. But in reality this has created a culture for all of us where we are contactable all the time, and we are not able to switch off. Downtime has been destroyed and more and more workers are suffering as a result of losing their work–life balance in this way. The problem has not gone unrecognised. At the beginning of 2017, France adopted a law giving workers the right to disconnect and not be contactable once home or within certain limits. Companies worldwide are beginning to acknowledge that workers need to be allowed to disconnect from their jobs to maintain their health and well-being.

I have seen often that it can be hard for overachievers and self-employed people particularly to appreciate that longer hours and overwork do not always correlate with success. So often people work harder and harder, running themselves into the ground, but not with the end result of greater productivity or greater success. Countless studies into effectiveness and productivity in fact reveal the converse to be true: fewer hours and active rest time is good not only for individual workers but also for companies. This is nothing new: Henry Ford showed this a century ago when he cut the working week in his factory from 48 to 40 hours and showed that working less did not harm his company.

The other thing that is difficult for overachievers and hard-workers in all roles to appreciate is that work–life balance is something they need to entertain. It is hard for highly motivated, successful and ambitious people to fathom, but we all need downtime. I see this particularly in men and women in their twenties, chasing their ambitions as they should be, but neglecting the rest of their lives. People who suffer with burnout, or any of the work-related health conditions, realise retrospectively that being successful in their career or job should not come at the price of abandoning what is important to them as a human – and, fundamentally, what is going to keep them healthy.

Shift Work

Currently over 3.5 million people in the UK have a work schedule where they are mainly doing shift work. As our lifestyles have become increasingly 24/7 and online, the range of jobs where shift work occurs has broadened from factory and essential services to include supermarket workers, call centre employees and even personal trainers in late night gyms. Large numbers of professions, such as the emergency services, lend themselves to shift work, which accounts for the vast numbers of employees either choosing or being forced into such work patterns.

There are known benefits to shift work: increased remuneration, flexible hours for family and childcare commitments, as well as some degree of choice in scheduling and routine, and days in lieu. But it has long been seen as a cause of work-related ill health, with many studies looking into the recognised association between shift work and poorer health.

There are fundamentally two areas that cause health problems from shift work. First, the lifestyle that ensues as a result of the abnormal hours is not healthy. Shift workers are away from their family and friends, and isolated more than most – a factor we know can be a cause of physical and mental ill health. There is a huge disruption to sleep patterns, resulting in overt insomnia or poor quality sleep which is detrimental both in the long and short term. Workers who do shift work for family reasons may forego sleep for childcare and family responsibilities, leading to chronic fatigue. Abnormal hours mean it can also be hard to foster the protective aspects of life such as exercise, proper relaxation time and a good diet. I know from my years as a junior doctor that vending machine snacks and late-night takeaways become your staple diet. It is hard to achieve work–life balance when you are living in a reverse world.

However, it is not only lifestyle that can be the problem. The second issue with shift work is the genuine physiological effects it has on the body. Humans are designed to be day-time creatures, with a daytime pattern of eating and being active and a night-time pattern of sleep. Our body clock has certain rhythms – known as circadian rhythms – influenced by hormones that govern a normal daytime pattern of activity and rest. For example, the stress hormone cortisol is highest in the morning, when we need to be alert, and low at night when we are programmed to sleep and relax. This internal body clock is regulated by external cues – daylight, mealtimes and clocks, for example – which keep us on this pattern with the world around us. Engaging in shift work disrupts this natural pattern and is thought to be the reason that shift work has been linked to a range of conditions, both physical and mental.

For example, even if you have the time and peace to sleep during the day, your body's hormones are prompting you to be active with a higher heart rate and blood pressure. Your sleep will be poorer in quality, so less restorative, and it is easy for insomnia to develop. Research shows that the higher rates of mental health problems in shift workers may not only be from the lifestyle and isolation they experience but also due to changes in brain chemistry that lead to lower levels of the mood chemical serotonin.

There is also evidence that associates long-term shift work with gastrointestinal problems such as irritable bowel syndrome, high blood pressure and increased vulnerability to recurrent minor illnesses. Not only that, it can also exacerbate existing issues such as diabetes and heart disease.

Shift work is not *guaranteed* to make people ill, of course – it is a risk. Shift workers can be protected by their own lifestyle, behaviour, age (it is easier when you are younger) and family, as well as the conditions they work in. There has been a huge amount of work done to identify the healthiest way to adopt shift work, looking at the length and make up of the shifts, how the rota moves and which activities are best undertaken during certain shifts. The physical environment of work can be protective – everything from the lighting and the temperature to the supervision and facilities you have. If these are all optimised, shift work does not have to come with the hefty price tag of ill health.

Emotionally Draining Jobs

A job that is emotionally draining and upsetting can easily take its toll on your health.

When you are emotionally involved in the lives, traumas and feelings of others it can impact on your own mental health and even worldview. Jobs such as social work and healthcare, as well as the police service, the military and teaching, have a very significant emotional component; dealing with death, pain, abuse or even just day-to-day human sadness will affect those undertaking them. Witnessing sights and situations that most of us can't even imagine amounts to trauma, and that trauma repeated over months and years in a professional role can have significant physical and mental health consequences. This does not just occur in the extreme scenario of the war reporter witnessing death and destruction, but even in the more benign settings of classrooms, call centres and care homes.

Being emotionally invested in the lives of others, being responsible for their well-being and care, as well as witnessing their pain and distress, makes a job mentally difficult. Not only that, it can easily become physically and mentally exhausting and debilitating.

I know from my own experience as a junior doctor and

then as a GP that there can be days when you are faced with life's worst scenarios. In my general practice recently I dealt with a case of child sexual abuse, then homelessness and finally a bereavement, all in the same day. Although they were not my own personal trauma, even the most experienced and hardened professionals will take on board some of that pain, which then goes on to affect your own mood. When such a pattern is repeated over and over again (as it can be in certain jobs such as social care or charity support work, where you are faced daily with distressing situations), a professional can unfortunately start to experience their own feelings of depression, pain and anger.

It does not matter how committed you are to your job. Many people with emotionally draining jobs are following their vocation and have the personality type suited to compassionate and caring roles. But they need to be very mindful of the effect that it can go on to have on them. I look after more than one charity worker who deals with the refugee crisis abroad, and coming face-to-face daily with the reality of what most of us just see as a flicker on the news is harrowing and traumatic. They have chosen to be in these roles and are compelled to do this tremendous work, but they are not immune to the psychological impact that it has on them.

Within these emotionally draining roles, it is even more essential to put in place strong protective factors to safeguard mental health – manageable workloads, good relationships and systems in place to enable workers to deal with the traumas they face. However, the reality is that usually these roles are found in the public sector or voluntary sector, where cash-strapped systems do not allow the essential coping mechanisms to be fostered. This is a common phenomenon within the charity sector, healthcare systems and social care. While big corporations can afford to offer their employees occupational health services, assistance programmes and health support, often where such help is most needed for workers it is sadly not feasible or available. Official figures for work-related ill health show that nurses and midwives have the highest rates of stress, followed by teachers: these are the classic examples of jobs with huge individual emotional investment and strain combined with the limited resources and high workload found within the public sector.

Of course many people within these roles manage a lifetime career of harrowing work which does not go on to make them ill. One cannot say exactly why that is, but protective factors would seem to be effective personal coping strategies, inherent emotional resilience, and an ability to compartmentalise and separate personal and professional lives. That often comes with experience, but it is also related to the work environment and the systems in place there, such as support, respite and a change of scene every once in a while.

Paradoxically, being in a caring profession does not always make for caring colleagues or managers. I have witnessed this often within medicine, where a hospital consultant can be fantastic at caring for his patients and their relatives, but totally lacks any empathy when it comes to caring for the well-being of his juniors, his nursing colleagues or his own secretary. It often seems that even though you work with caring professionals, you can't necessarily expect to get looked after yourself.

Wrong Place, Wrong Time, Wrong Job

While not strictly speaking a documented cause of ill health, there are people who suffer from their job because they are simply in the wrong job at the wrong time.

By necessity there are many people undertaking jobs with poor salaries, difficult commutes or a mismatch between the role and their personal skills set. Of course this is going to be unsatisfying and, I would hypothesise, for some it will lead to ill health. Being forced to travel more than you like, being away from family, or undertaking lengthy and tiresome commutes will impact a degree on mental health. Likewise, if someone feels undervalued in taking a role that is beneath their skills set, or is forced through financial circumstances to take a contract on poor terms, their self-esteem and self-worth will be knocked.

Unlike the other causes of job-related illness this is not simply a work-related issue, but rather a mismatch of job and person creating the negative position.

Short term, and often as part of a career ladder, this happens to many of us when we're starting our working lives, and is perhaps acceptable at a younger age. But it is unsatisfying and mentally draining to be in this position long term, or later in life when you may be forced into the situation, for example, if you need to start again after a job loss. Whatever the circumstances, it is very hard to accept the status quo of being in the wrong job.

Recognising the Cause of Your Own Work-related Ill Health

It is so important for you to understand the factors that have caused your own work-related ill health from the potential situations that I have outlined in this chapter.

For many people, even recognising these issues at work is not straightforward. Of course, it is easy to see when you are faced with an overtly bullying boss or a difficult colleague, but for people who love their job and feel they need stress in order to achieve, or those who have got their work–life balance just a bit wrong but are muddling through, the notion that your job could be making you ill seems almost far-fetched.

This is not surprising. Work is a significant part of an adult's life: it bestows our sense of achievement, success, pride, socio-economic status and self-esteem, and is far more than 'just a job' for most people. Admitting that it could all be in jeopardy is therefore very, very hard.

Whatever has brought you to this book, whether it is one of the common issues outlined in this chapter, or something more specific, a fundamental basis for your recovery, resolution or cure, no matter what the circumstances, is to acknowledge the issue.

Even with the simplest ailment or problem, you have to start with acknowledgement: a straightforward thought process that will enable you to accept the current state of affairs and take steps to improve your situation. In the simplest of terms it would go something like this: 'I seem to have symptoms of a runny nose, sneezing and a sore throat; I must have a cold; I will get some paracetamol and rest.' Your mind does this hundreds of times a day and of course each time you will not consciously go through these steps; but the steps have happened, albeit fluidly and subconsciously, in order for you to focus your attention in the right way and take the appropriate actions.

While obviously simple for diagnosing your own cold, acknowledgement can be very tough when it comes to diagnosing any work-related ill health and accepting it. There are a number of reasons for this:

• Many of us, understandably, don't want to accept that work-related illness could be the issue: it seems like such a gargantuan subject to face, naturally we would prefer to see an alternative, simpler cause.

- Your symptoms may not be stark or at crisis-point but be mild and more insidious in their onset. This makes the problem harder to see if it has gradually started and almost become your new normal, before you have had the chance to realise what is going on.

- It is difficult to accept any illness and take on the 'sick role', whether the problem is physical or psychological.

- Acknowledging the issue exists means it has become concrete and you have to face the mammoth task of dealing with it.

- It can be very hard to understand that work or a job – which is something that the majority of adults undertake and is therefore the norm – is actually something that can cause illness for you as an individual.

- It is embarrassing to admit that work is making you ill.

- It feels like a weakness to admit that work is making you ill.

Chapters 2 and 3 will explore some of the most common health issues brought about by the workplace situations covered in this chapter. Together these chapters will help you to accept and build up a picture of what you are going through, help you to acknowledge them and begin the process of recovery.

•

CHAPTER 2

Job-related Mental Illness

Your next step is to recognise the illness you are suffering from, and to understand the correct treatment you need. This is a fundamental part of accepting your job-related ill health.

In the last decade, without question, I have mostly seen work-related ill health in the form of mental health symptoms and conditions. Figures show problems at work are more likely to cause psychological issues than physical ones. From the patients I have met myself over the years, it is far easier for them to equate psychological symptoms such as low mood to their work than it is to recognise it as being related to a physical issue, such as stomach pains. So perhaps as doctor and patient, we have made the diagnosis easier and sooner when the problem is psychological. With physical health conditions, as you will see in the next chapter, it is harder to see that link with work.

The range of problems which can be caused by your job can be classified into well-defined diagnoses and illnesses, but all have the common trait of being precipitated by a work environment or the lifestyle associated with it.

With all psychological illnesses or mental health conditions, whether related to work or otherwise, there is a degree of stigma and unnecessary guilt that comes with a diagnosis. This sadly results from the lack of awareness that mental health campaigners are fighting to change, and the fact that the dialogue around mental health still lags behind that around physical health. A vast amount of my daily work as a GP is around the mental health of people – anyone can have a mental illness. It is certainly not a weakness, and in my mind seeking help for depression is no different from seeking help for diabetes.

Mental health conditions can be hard to recognise, and that is not simply down to a lack of awareness. They can have a slow, insidious start rather than a dramatic, explosive onset. Patients will often tell me that they feel their symptoms crept up on them slowly and gradually, without them realising for a few months what was actually happening. Although mental health symptoms can be very clear for a doctor to see and define, those same signs can be hard to acknowledge and appreciate from the patient's viewpoint.

The symptoms often start quietly and gently, and people grow accustomed to a new norm – for example, the broken nights' sleep or lack of interest in having fun. Until the signs are more extensive or more severe, it can be hard to appreciate what is going on. It is often a comment from a relative or friend that precipitates someone to seek help, or a crisis when symptoms become so dramatic that they are impossible to ignore. By then, unfortunately, there can already be a significant and moderately severe condition embedded, which may be harder to treat.

The most common mental health issues and conditions we see in GP surgeries as a result of jobs and work are:

- Stress

- Anxiety

- Panic attacks

- Depression

- Addiction

- Relationship breakdowns

An overview of each condition is given below, to help you understand what each can look like and the treatment you should be getting. Although you need to deal with issues from work and instigate lifestyle changes, fundamentally you need to diagnose and treat your illness. This comes now.

Stress

The word 'stress' feels very overused. It is often thrown around in any context and pinned to even the most banal and irrelevant situations.

However, in the context of job-related ill health it is far from overused. In 2015/16 stress accounted for 37 per cent of all work-related ill health cases in the UK, and for as much as 45 per cent of all working days lost due to ill health. For every 100,000 workers, 1,230 will be affected by stress. It is a significant issue for sure. The inappropriate overuse of the word in daily life belittles just how extensive and significant the issue can be and as a result has sadly done a disservice to those suffering.

Small amounts of stress are a normal part of daily life for everyone, and can in fact be a good thing. We all at times use stress, and the impetus it brings, to keep going – a boost to perk us up and push us forward to those goals. Everyone experiences that and it can certainly be a force for good for many of us, in both our professional and personal lives.

In fact, many workers thrive on stress and almost need it to motivate and achieve. You will hear high achievers often say that stress drives them, encourages them and pushes them to get results and succeed in life. Having pressure, deadlines, responsibilities are a normal part of life for everyone, and feeling stressed is a normal part of that.

Our bodies are used to some stress and are designed for it: the body makes specific stress hormones – cortisol and adrenalin – in response to physical and emotional stressors. So whether you are running away from danger, or running through an airport to catch a flight, you will be making these hormones. We often refer to these as the 'flight or fight hormones'. This is the body's natural way of preparing literally for a fight, a threat or a danger. Producing those hormones in response gets you ready for whatever action is needed.

The fight-or-flight feeling is fine – and is vital if you are a caveman and need to be prepared at any time to run away from a bear. The problems arise for us twenty-first-century humans when those hormones are produced throughout the day, multiple times through the week, essentially leaving you on a constant high state of alert waiting for the next threat. That can be what stress feels like.

Stress becomes a problem when that heightened state of alert starts to take over: the overwhelming feeling that you experience is the stress itself, rather than enjoyment or triumph or any sense of relaxation. So, thinking about our high achiever who loves and thrives on stress, rather than enjoying the achievements and successes he has been driven to, he can only feel the fight-or-flight response. This is representative of stress becoming a problem.

Although we can all recognise that feeling of stress or

finding something stressful, it can be hard to define it as an issue. Formally, stress is not a medical diagnosis. Unlike depression and anxiety and the other mental health problems, it doesn't have diagnostic symptoms and set criteria a doctor can use to make a diagnosis. But it is a recognised issue and, as we have seen, a hugely common one with significant consequences in terms of working-days lost. After bereavement and divorce, jobs are the third-biggest cause of stress.

Symptoms

Stress within the context of job-related ill health can be recognised by some of the following characteristics:

- Feeling there is so much to think about, it stops you concentrating on the single task at hand.

- Your mind is racing with all the deadlines and tasks you need to do, and it feels like a nebulous hurdle rather than easy-to-define tasks to complete.

- Feeling out of control with deadlines or your work situation and finding that feeling uncomfortable (obviously there are times in our life when we feel out of control and it is enjoyable).

- Not coping or being able to achieve demands or objectives asked of you at work – you feel overburdened.

- Finding it hard to make decisions at work.

- Feeling uncertainty about tomorrow and the future, and perhaps dreading it.

- Feeling under pressure and trapped by the situation or demands on you.

- Feeling like something is going to go dreadfully wrong.

- Constantly feeling nervous, experiencing butterflies or feeling tense.

- Not being able to switch off from your work tasks and relax, no matter where you are or when it is, for example a weekend morning.

No matter what the cause, stress can elicit a wider spectrum of symptoms that may occur in conjunction with any of the characteristics above:

- Thoughts racing through your head when you are trying to sleep

- Feeling irritable with no justifiable cause

- Feeling sick or tense in the stomach

- Thumping heart

- Increasing your smoking or alcohol habits

Although stress is not a defined medical diagnosis, it is certainly recognised and appreciated by the medical profession as something that needs sympathy, help and (possibly) therapeutic intervention. It is well known as being, for some patients, the first step towards a more concrete mental health problem such as depression or anxiety. It can also be an isolated issue that resolves without any further progression.

There is no set pathway in terms of treatment for stress, but that certainly doesn't mean there is no help available. Indeed, much of the impetus for this book was because there are in fact so many ways to help and deal with work stress which in itself can be overwhelming.

The mainstay of treatment for stress is arranging your

working life to reduce stress through lifestyle changes and holistic stress reduction. Your exercise routine, your caffeine intake and your time spent relaxing with friends will all help to reduce symptoms of stress. These are explained fully (with all the self-driven lifestyle changes) in Chapter 6.

As well as lifestyle changes and focused self-help, stress can require medical input: this can be in the form of therapy or medication. Medical treatment can be necessary because the stress has tipped over into significant insomnia or low mood, or the stress symptoms themselves are so distressing and life changing and require assertive help. This is not to underestimate the power of the lifestyle changes recommended, but extra medical input may be required in addition. Medical treatment can seem like a big leap to take but it can be valuable to break the negative cycle that develops from untreated stress.

In terms of therapy, stress can reduce with talking therapy as you are encouraged to deal with the thoughts and feelings that arise from your stress, and halt those damaging thought processes. Stress responds well to cognitive behavioural therapy (CBT) – detailed in the next section on anxiety. Mindfulness-based stress reduction (MBSR) is a specific therapy focused solely on stress, incorporating the elements of mindfulness, exercise and meditation. Both can be accessed online (see Resources, page 216) or in face-to-face therapy sessions.

Medication would be prescribed for stress only in very specific situations, on a case-by-case basis (as all medicines should be), because stress doesn't have specific pharmaceutical treatment guidelines. It can be essential, however, to consider a prescription for medications to help resolve sleep issues or to control anxiety. Occasionally an antidepressant may be prescribed at a lower therapeutic dose to take the edge off the stress symptoms, curbing the distressing highs and lows that can occur.

Anxiety

Feeling worried or being anxious about a specific event or issue is totally normal. It is a standard part of a busy life, and an ordinary part of working life. It is quite clearly perfectly rational and reasonable to feel worried before giving a presentation, when you take on a new role or when your line manager changes. Worry is a normal human emotional response to fear and the unknown, and we can all recognise it in ourselves.

Anxiety becomes an illness when it occurs so often or for so long that it actually interferes with your life, your enjoyment and your achievements, and even your simple mundane activities. The anxiety feelings themselves are so strong that they become overwhelming.

Symptoms

Anxiety is a recognised mental health condition with specific diagnostic criteria. It can be called generalised anxiety disorder or GAD. Feeling anxious is to feel worried, nervous, tense and even fearful; this becomes full-blown anxiety when these feelings stop you getting on with your working day or specific activities, such as getting yourself on the bus to work or even making yourself a sandwich.

It is possible your anxiety could be a diagnosable illness if it is characterised by these certain specific features that would occur on the majority of days in the week:

- You constantly worry, feel nervous or feel on edge.

- You don't feel able to stop yourself worrying or control it.

- The worry itself upsets you or stresses you out.

- The worry stops you doing normal things including work and pleasurable activities.

- You experience wide-ranging worries, from the trivial to weighty issues.

- You find yourself catastrophising – thinking the worst will happen for any eventuality.

- Your worries stop you relaxing.

- You feel restless, irritable and are easily annoyed.

Anxiety disorder can have physical as well as the above psychological symptoms. The way we feel when we are anxious arises in part of the brain known as the amygdala, an area in charge of emotion, emotional behaviour and survival instinct. The body comes under the influence of our fight-or-flight hormone, adrenalin, preparing for battle. As such we not only feel anxiety emotionally, we feel it physically as our body prepares for action: the heart rate increases and breathing quickens. The physical symptoms will be familiar to anyone who has felt nervous about a job interview or a big change.

Beyond just simply 'feeling worried', the symptoms of anxiety disorders include the following extensive range of physical and psychological symptoms:

- Nervousness, worry or tension

- Restlessness

- A sense of dread

- Irritability

- Social withdrawal

- Palpitations or thumping heartbeats

- Headaches

- Dizziness

- Aches and pains

- Dry mouth

- Fast breathing

- Feeling sick

- Insomnia – both difficulty falling asleep and difficulty staying asleep

There is a huge range of symptoms that anxiety can cause and it may be that only a few are present. It is very important to realise that some of these can be features of other diagnoses, including severe physical conditions such as heart and lung disease, or thyroid problems, so it is vital that they are assessed and evaluated properly by a doctor.

Whether you have many symptoms of anxiety or just a couple, if your daily life is affected or you are distressed by your anxiety, then you need help. Essentially what is important to recognise are whether these symptoms are taking hold and taking control of your life, so that they have become the overwhelming feeling masking happiness, pleasure or calm.

Diagnosing anxiety formally is essential for affirmation and acceptance by sufferers, and it is fundamental to formulating a therapeutic plan. Sometimes it is very clear to a doctor that anxiety is the issue, particularly if you are presenting with months or years of symptoms that easily fit the criteria. But occasionally it can be harder with the more insidious symptoms – perhaps with a predominance of physical symptoms that may be confused with a bowel problem – or at the early stages of the disease when your symptoms are still very mild or infrequent. Healthcare professionals would be loath to make a long-term diagnosis of anxiety for what could be a transient and temporary issue that has lasted a week or two, so it may be that a definitive diagnosis takes more than one consultation over a couple of months. You may be asked to have a more formal assessment with a psychiatrist, or to fill out a questionnaire about symptoms and how often you are experiencing them. This can be very useful to determine an accurate diagnosis.

Treatment

Along with the holistic lifestyle changes which will be outlined in Chapter 6, treatment of anxiety will generally always look at talking-therapy options before medication options. In my anecdotal experience, I wouldn't say one is better or worse than the other, or that the combination of both is the right way. With a patient in front of me, we often find there isn't actually a choice: sometimes people can't tolerate medication, for example, or they can't get to therapy, meaning they have to rely on the other treatment options. It is not uncommon for me to hear from patients with work-related anxiety that they don't have time for therapy because of their job – a real catch-22. It is always worth exploring all the options though, and being fully informed about what is available to you in terms of treatment. Knowledge is certainly power when it comes to treating a mental health issue.

Cognitive behavioural therapy (CBT) is the most well-known and well-established type of therapy for anxiety. CBT helps people change the way they think and the way they behave. Studies show that it helps control anxiety in around half of those who receive the therapy for the condition, reducing the daily symptoms and improving quality of life. It is a very goal-based therapy designed to change your behaviour and affect change in your life going forward. It is not the type of therapy that analyses the past or what has happened, so it would not delve into your childhood experiences or situations at work to look for the root of the problem. However, at the outset the therapist would explore these causes, but only in order to work towards changing the behaviours and thoughts that occur as a result of these negative situations.

During CBT you are encouraged to understand your thoughts, particularly the unhelpful and harmful ones that make you feel anxious, so that you can change those thought processes and improve your state of mind.

How we think affects our feelings and then how we behave and act. Changing unhelpful and harmful behaviours which arise from negative thoughts is the focus of CBT, so you effectively learn how to stop recurring destructive and distressing behaviour patterns. It is a very active type of therapy and it is usual to be given homework to trial strategies and actions on your own – replacing anxious thoughts with helpful ones in your day-to-day life. CBT is usually offered in a face-to-face setting or online, and should occur weekly or fortnightly for many months. While we know it is certainly effective, it is not a quick-fix treatment, as it takes many sessions, and you can find yourself more anxious in the initial phase as you confront your anxieties and worries.

Medications are commonly used for anxiety and may be as effective as therapy. For anyone starting medication, weighing up the benefits and the side-effects is crucial and should involve a detailed chat with your doctor. Antidepressants are the medications most commonly prescribed for anxiety. Doctors used to use a lot of tranquilliser drugs such as diazepam, but these are addictive and mind-numbing and have, thankfully, been mostly replaced by the wider use of antidepressants, which have a good scientific evidence-base behind them.

Antidepressants used to treat anxiety are usually the type known as SSRIs – selective serotonin reuptake inhibitors – which alter the levels of mood-changing chemicals in the brain, the neurotransmitters. They are not addictive (unlike their predecessors), but they can take time to be effective, and you have to stick with them through an often difficult first few weeks as their effects build up. You should be closely monitored during this time by your doctor and your family as your anxiety can actually increase in the first few days.

If the physical symptoms of anxiety are the most predominant, it may be that a beta-blocker such as propranolol is suggested. These medications directly work on the heart and slow down the heart rate, controlling the pulse-racing and heart-thumping effects of anxiety. Reducing this physical effect is known to reduce the anxiety felt psychologically.

Panic Attacks

Panic attacks are a very frightening physical and psychological experience, when the body experiences an overpowering sense of fear and dread. Panic attacks are a common issue, thought to affect over 1 per cent of the population in the UK. Within my general practice, I am very accustomed to hearing about them from patients whose job is making them ill. The build up of anxiety that can arise from job situations, coupled with the unrelenting routine of working in a detrimental environment, can undoubtedly precipitate panic attacks in someone susceptible. Panic attacks go hand-in-hand with anxiety but they are a separate entity to the anxiety symptoms I have already described: people with panic attacks may not have other regular significant symptoms of anxiety. Likewise, it is very possible to have anxiety without having panic attacks.

The feelings experienced during a panic attack are so overwhelming that I have frequently heard patients describe the moment of the attack by saying 'I thought I was having a heart attack', or 'I actually felt I was dying'. One teacher I used to look after genuinely felt during her first attack that she was having a stroke: that is how shocking and paralysing the sensation can be.

Symptoms

Panic attacks are a tangible, physical manifestation of a psychological condition. The physical symptoms are so intense it can be hard to appreciate that they have a psychological origin. It can also be a particularly inconvenient and embarrassing condition: patients of mine have been struck by a panic attack on public transport, in work meetings, before vital presentations and even at an office Christmas party.

'Panic disorder' is the term we use when someone has panic attacks regularly. The condition is related to anxiety but, specifically with panic, you feel your symptoms in huge waves, very suddenly and unexpectedly. It is literally an 'attack', with strong physical and psychological symptoms coming on rapidly. Attacks can occur repeatedly and regularly. The overwhelming emotional feeling is of dread and fear (literally panic), combined with intense physical symptoms such as:

- Feeling your heart is beating rapidly, very strongly or irregularly

- Breathing very quickly or feeling you can't catch your breath quickly enough

- Sweating and feeling a flush of heat through your body

- Dizziness and feeling faint

- Shaking, trembling, teeth-chattering or shivering

- Chest pain

- Nausea

- Pins and needles, tingling and numbness particularly in the fingers

- Feeling your mouth go intensely dry

A panic attack may last only 5 minutes, or as many as 20. Because of the very sudden onset and severe nature of panic-attack symptoms, many who have experienced them find themselves receiving emergency help from paramedics, a first aider in a public place, or in A&E. Particularly the first time, it can be hard to distinguish a panic attack from an acute physical emergency such as a heart attack. A formal diagnosis is straightforward to make as the symptoms are so apparent and definitive, but it can be important to rule out cardiac and lung conditions given how significant the heart and breathing changes can be.

Treatment

People with panic disorder learn techniques to cope with the moment of the attack. The attack will stop by itself, so sufferers can use coping mechanisms to see out the attack.

These involve breathing, focusing, staying safe and positive visualisation techniques. These are simple self-management strategies to help control the attack and lessen the enormity of the palpable symptoms. The attack will end by itself and, as long as you are in a safe place, will cause no physical harm.

In the longer term, treatment of panic disorder should involve cognitive behavioural therapy (CBT) as it is recognised as an incredibly effective psychological treatment for the condition. Regular sessions over two to four months will help you address the negative thoughts that can lead to the panic attacks, replacing them with positive, less damaging ones. In turn this leads to the adaptation of your patterns of behaviour and less frequent attacks.

Given the very intense nature of the physical symptoms of panic it is unsurprising that many people feel they need medication to control the condition. For panic, just as with other anxiety disorders, the scientific evidence suggests therapy is superior to medication. But medication is available for panic and follows the same line of treatments that we use in anxiety (see pages 44–5). Sufferers of panic attacks can feel they need something to control the physical symptoms, such as a beta-blocker or tranquilliser as a pill-in-their-pocket insurance policy to cope, particularly at the moment of terror. One of the issues with this, however, is that while a panic attack may last 20 minutes, the effects of any medication may last hours and can be more inconvenient and disruptive than the attack itself.

Depression

Feeling a bit down at times for a justified reason (or in fact even for no reason) is so common, it is essentially normal. Everyone in every stage of life and every job has days of feeling low, or a bit depressed, or generally a bit fed up. The end of a holiday and Sunday nights particularly are bad, of course, as are those occasional days when you wished you had applied for that promotion or didn't have to work with a particular colleague. The odd day experiencing unhappiness is completely standard for us all, whether employed or not. This is obviously not a sign of being unwell.

Depression is completely different from that.

Fundamentally, the difference between feeling low and a diagnosis of the mental health condition depression is that depression symptoms will occur on most days, and will continue the same for a few weeks. There are very recognisable and distinctive symptoms of depression and these become the overwhelming feeling you experience all the time, no matter where you are and what you are doing.

Like any mental health condition, depression is a very significant diagnosis. Particularly for someone who is working, responsible for the family income or high up the office hierarchy, it often comes with feelings of inadequacy, guilt and shame. It is sad that these feelings prevail, but they do because our culture is still not quite au fait with the concept of mental health. That is particularly surprising given that 1 in 10 people will suffer with depression at some point in their lives and it affects both sexes and all ages. Unfortunately, and sometimes critically, there is a reluctance to accept help or treatment.

Because of the hesitancy to acknowledge mental health diagnoses, but also because the symptoms can be rather vague and subtle initially, depression can occasionally occur without people appreciating what is going on. This is something I have seen commonly in general practice: patients with depression who don't particularly acknowledge their depression symptoms but attend a clinic with other symptoms, such as poor sleep or appetite changes.

Symptoms

The symptoms of depression can vary widely, as can how severely people are affected. Sufferers find these symptoms last for weeks or months, and will interfere with all aspects of life, both professional and social. The recognised symptoms of depression include:

- Ongoing sadness and low mood

- Feeling tearful and hopeless

- Low self-esteem, feeling like a failure or feeling useless

- Feeling guilty about the way you feel

- Finding it hard to concentrate and make decisions

- Lacking motivation to do anything

- Thinking life is not worth living

- Waking up very early in the morning and not getting back to sleep

- Losing enjoyment in activities you previously enjoyed such as hobbies and socialising

- Withdrawing from socialising

- Feeling easily irritated for little reason

- Losing interest in food, forgetting to eat or no longer enjoying a meal

- Losing interest in your relationship and sex

- Feeling fatigued and lacking energy

Diagnosing depression usually involves a very probing consultation with your doctor. It is absolutely crucial to get the diagnosis right – depression can mimic other mental health conditions and also other physical health conditions such as thyroid disease, so a thorough assessment is vital. Doctors often use score tests to evaluate symptoms and seek to quantify the duration and severity of the symptoms you are experiencing. It is normal to be asked about suicidal thoughts, feelings of self-worth and your relationship.

People from all walks of life and with all sorts of jobs have told me time and time again that they are scared to admit they could have depression, delaying them seeking the diagnosis and treatment they need. There is a concern about becoming addicted to antidepressants, a fear of being judged and a reluctance to admit to a perceived weakness. In fact, the truth is that antidepressants are generally not addictive nowadays, people are no longer universally judged for having a mental health problem as they once were, and depression is no more a weakness than developing arthritis.

More than one employee I have seen has been concerned that somehow our discussion in the consultation room could be leaked to their employer or that their company could seek their private health information. The conversations you have with your doctor remain confidential, and this confidentiality would only ever be breached in very extreme circumstances – if you were a risk to yourself or others. If, for insurance purposes, your health records are requested by an outside agency, they can only ever be disclosed with your consent, including your agreement about what exact diagnoses are included.

Treatment

Treating depression early can really improve your prognosis and your chances of full recovery. The earlier in the disease you start treatment, the higher the chance of it working because you should be in the milder stages before your mood falls further and damaging thoughts and behaviours have become ingrained.

As with anxiety, as well as the lifestyle changes to improve your work-related health (see Chapter 6), the treatment of depression falls into the two categories of medication and talking therapy. This is a familiar triad within mental health conditions: the self-help lifestyle treatment you undertake yourself, along with prescribed medication and therapy, work together to bring about recovery and remission.

Antidepressants are the usual medicine prescribed for depression and there is a huge range now available to be prescribed. Most commonly we use medicines called SSRIs – selective serotonin reuptake inhibitors – including sertraline, citalopram and fluoxetine. These are the medications that studies recommend most highly as the most effective, with the least side-effects. These would really be the entry-level antidepressants: there are many other types now used by psychiatrists for severe and resistant depression, but these would only be tried after several others had failed.

The antidepressant suggested for you will depend on your specific symptoms, your background health and how severe your doctor feels the depression is. Starting a new medicine is always a reason for an in-depth discussion with your doctor about its pros and cons as well as the long-term outlook. Even more so with an antidepressant: it is a big step to start a medication for depression, as it becomes a very tangible way of accepting you have a mental health condition. That in itself can feel like a big leap, but it is worth it for many. Studies show that many of the symptoms of depression will be relieved by antidepressants. Although they cannot alter the issues you are facing at work, relieving even some of the more distressing symptoms can allow you to foster some of your own changes and improve your chances of dealing with the difficult times.

The main problem with starting an antidepressant can come in the first few days, when you can in fact feel worse in terms of your mood. It is crucial that you are aware of this and have support from those around you. After the initial period, an antidepressant will take up to four weeks to build up its effects to the point where changes in symptoms would be clearly seen. If no change is evident, it would be standard practice to increase the dose now or try an alternative drug. Antidepressants are not addictive and generally do not sedate people (like the older types formerly used), which is crucial for someone who needs to carry on functioning and performing in a job.

Therapy also has a substantial role to play in the management of depression. Many forms are known to work well for the illness; there is as strong a scientific basis for the talking therapies as there is for the medicines, so therapies are not to be considered a second-rate option. As discussed in the section on anxiety, CBT is commonly used and well recognised as being an effective treatment for depression. It can be offered in different ways: one on one; in groups; face to face; or online. The range of options is there so that you can opt for something you will be able to stick with. CBT can last for at least eight sessions, over a period of weeks and months. That is a big commitment and it is worth being honest at the outset about what you can realistically sign up for, which is why online and computer-based self-help CBT have recently become so popular for people with busy working lives.

Interpersonal therapy is a type of therapy where you focus on your dealings with others and events in your life. It can also be useful for depression when it is thought that the depression is exacerbated and precipitated by personal relationships: it allows you to change your thinking and behaviour and your interactions with others. As we saw in Chapter 1, your personal relationships can be very relevant to work-related ill health.

Psychodynamic psychotherapy is another type of psycho-analysis that may be used for depression, where you explore your thoughts and behaviours and their origins. This can help to elicit why you may have developed patterns of behaviour throughout your life that are detrimental to yourself. A combination of this and CBT is offered by some psychotherapists: this is known as cognitive analytical therapy or CAT.

Finally, counselling is not to be dismissed. While it is the 'mildest' form of therapy it can be the easiest and cheapest to access. It is not therapy per se, but is ideal for people who need the chance to think about the issues, talk openly and confidentially, and need support finding practical solutions. It can be valuable for someone with 'mild' depression.

Addiction

As many as 1 in 3 adults could be addicted to something. Addicts are by no means an obvious homogeneous group, limited to our stereotyped picture of a 'druggie' or an alcoholic. Addicts come in many guises and many are in suits and uniforms, holding down responsible jobs, with families and careers, and are far, far removed from any typecast addict we all imagine.

There are many theories as to what causes addiction, but in my own opinion it is a combination of factors: some genetic tendency, most likely coupled with a response to life situations or trauma, as well as social groupings. In someone with a predisposition to addiction, a difficult working life could easily provide the trigger to an addiction: as a way of dealing with the stress or the emotional pain; as a coping mechanism; as a distraction; or even as a misguided way to relax after a terrible day in the office.

Symptoms

Addiction is commonly associated with alcohol and drugs, but there is a huge range of addictions including to nicotine, street drugs, prescribed drugs, over-the-counter painkillers, pornography, gambling, sex, shopping and solvents. The defining features of any addiction are that you have no control to stop seeking out your particular addiction and do so to the point of risk and harm to yourself. These risks and harms can be financial ruin or divorce just as easily as they can be physical ill health and decline. The fallout from addictions can be enormous, both in terms of psychological and physical effects as well as the far-reaching effect on work, family and social life. It is not an exaggeration to say that addiction can be life-destroying: it is by no means a trivial problem.

Addiction across all types is characterised by compulsion, and while we all at times feel addicted to something pleasurable, having addiction as a condition has far more substantial symptoms. A combination of these would be present for a formal diagnosis to be made:

- Feeling uncontrollably compelled to carry on the addictive behaviour

- Trying at least once to have stopped without success

- Needing more and more of the addiction to satisfy your needs

- Physical and mood changes when you can't satisfy the addiction; for example in the case of drugs, withdrawal symptoms, or in the case of gambling, changes in mood and restlessness

- Continuing the addiction despite health and personal risks such as financial risks

- Sacrificing social, personal and family life to meet the addiction

- Addiction-seeking behaviour: always ensuring your addiction needs will be met no matter where you are or when it is, and obsessing over your constant supply

- Feeling guilty about your addiction despite wanting to carry on

- Engaging in secrecy to meet your addiction needs

Treatment

Seeking help for an addiction is very hard, and often only happens at a crisis point – the loss of a relationship, the loss of a job or a health watershed leads people to seek help. Addiction itself is characterised by shame and secrecy, which can prevent people seeking help early when they need it and when treatment can be more successful.

Recovery from addiction is multifaceted. In the case of substance abuse – whether drugs or alcohol – this needs to be managed by a doctor to ensure the safe stopping of medication, avoiding potentially dangerous withdrawal symptoms and managing any physical health issues such as liver damage. Anyone seeking to give up a substance addiction should seek advice from a professional to ensure all the health issues have been addressed. In the case of drugs or severe alcoholism this could involve engaging in a formal detoxification programme.

Support is the key to a good recovery, and I would advise anyone trying to recover from an addiction to find a formal support network or self-help group: 12-step programmes such as that of Alcoholics Anonymous, or self-management programmes such as SMART (Self-Management and Recovery Training), are renowned for their success in this area. Their value is endorsed by medical guidelines which verify their place within the recognised treatment of addiction. There are networks available online as well as face to face worldwide, making their peer support unrivalled in terms of availability and therefore success. It can be a daunting process to start, but worth it to engage in a proven method of treatment.

In terms of psychological therapy, addictions of all types respond well to CBT. CBT focuses on damaging thoughts; these are very prevalent for addicts and lead to the continuing patterns of damaging behaviour that ensue. Courses of CBT help to alter those thoughts and instil more valuable ones, thus altering the subsequent destructive addictive behaviour. Using therapy coupled with a support network is shown by research to be the most successful strategy for addiction recovery.

Relationship Breakdown

Is it right to call divorce an illness?

The answer is no, of course, but although it would be wrong to classify divorce as a mental health condition, relationship breakdowns sadly deserve their place in this book about work-related ill health. Relationships form a vital underpinning of our overall health and their breakdown can be detrimental to both physical and mental needs. It has not been uncommon for me over the last few years to see patients suffering with work-related stress or anxiety and experiencing relationship breakdown as part of the fallout.

The different ways people respond to stress and the

different symptoms they suffer can easily affect marriages and relationships. Relationships will be rocked if someone lacks their usual motivation or enjoyment of fun, as they often do with stress, and particularly if they withdraw from their partner and stop opening up, which can be common. I have also seen the opposite situation, when the irritability and anger from stress causes volatility, confrontation and a very turbulent home life that eventually becomes unworkable. When hours meant for home life are dedicated to overtime, thinking about work or feeling ill from work, that neglected relationship is going to suffer.

In addition, we must not forget the impact stress and overwork will have on libido, sexual function and fertility: these fundamental aspects of a relationship can be affected by your work, adding even more pressure to a relationship. On more than one occasion I have treated male patients for new-onset erectile dysfunction when the only obvious precipitating factor they can cite is work-related stress; colleagues within IVF clinics have seen the same problem affecting fertility.

Work-related stress can have a very negative impact on all relationships – not just partners but parents and children too. Healthy relationships are crucial for well-being and need the attention and TLC that your mental and physical health get when they are damaged. Many of the lifestyle changes suggested in Chapter 6 will help protect, nourish and even repair relationships.

The aim of this chapter has to been to outline the mental health conditions that you may be suffering from as a result of your job.

Understanding what your symptoms mean and what treatment you should seek is vital to your ongoing recovery. I have always believed in giving patients 'health literacy' – knowledge of conditions and potential treatments, so that they can play an active and informed role in their own healing. This is absolutely vital when your work is making you ill; you are the driver behind your own recovery and to do that you need to understand your illness. This is how you will access the correct treatment and build a healthy path into the future.

●

CHAPTER 3

Job-related Physical Illness

Over my years in general practice the job-related illness I have seen has not only manifested as mental health conditions and overt stress. Many of the patients I have seen have developed physical illnesses or symptoms rather than explicitly psychological ones.

There are, of course, ailments and issues you may expect as direct consequences of the physical constraints or activities you do in your work. If you are a builder, you probably anticipate some physical aches and pains as a result of the job, just like footballers expect dodgy knees. My optician told me that after years of bending over to looking closely into people's eyes, she suffers with neck and back problems that are so significant that she requires physiotherapy. But there are a whole group of people who suffer with job-related physical health problems that should *not* be part and parcel of their role or an expected consequence, but arise from the negative work-related issues covered in Chapter 1 and the consequent mental health problems highlighted in Chapter 2.

Our minds and bodies are very closely related, and within the area of work-related ill health it has been common for me to see patients with conditions affecting all parts of the body when the cause is a negative work situation. Job-related physical illness is a hard diagnosis to make, as our automatic position is to relate physical illness to a physical or physiological problem, and it can be hard for both patient and doctor to see an alternative origin. It is made even more difficult as doctors often see patients who report physical symptoms such as insomnia or headaches, but who deny or omit to mention that they feel stressed or anxious as well.

Case Study

Several years ago I looked after a man who worked as a teacher in an adult education college. I saw him for his blood pressure treatment for which he needed regular review and monitoring. It was relatively hard to keep his blood pressure controlled and he needed three types of tablets daily to achieve this. He was in his late fifties, relatively slim and active and seemed to enjoy family life and social activities as well as work. He mentioned work from time to time but very much in passing; for example if he was running late for an appointment: it was hectic but hugely satisfying, sometimes there weren't enough staff, at one point he took on a bit of management responsibility as well as teaching. Just snippets here and there, all said with a smile on his face talking about a job he clearly relished and that very much defined him as a person. It isn't normal for someone to need three blood pressure medications, but as we had ruled out serious physical causes of resistant high blood pressure such as kidney disease, we continued the treatment and it worked – until a few years later when he started to feel dizzy with the medication.

He came back to the clinic early and his blood pressure was now too low, causing the dizziness. This remained the trend for a week or two and we decided to try continuing just two of the medications. 'You know, I've gone part time at work before I retire next year,' he told me while I printed the new prescription regime. I asked if he thought that would explain the blood pressure changes: less stress and so naturally his blood pressure had reduced (as we know stress has a direct effect on blood pressure). He didn't think so, and to be honest nor did I really, as he just didn't fit that stereotype of someone stressed out by their job, as he always told me how much he liked it. Eighteen months later, when he retired, he was back with me in the clinic and we took him down to just one tablet, which controlled his blood pressure easily. We could both finally acknowledge the impact his job had had on his blood pressure over the years, which was only really possible to see with the benefit of time and once his work pattern had dramatically changed.

The Relationship Between the Mind and Physical Symptoms

It can be difficult to accept that a physical issue has a psychological or emotional root cause, however this happens throughout our lives. Even from childhood we can notice the physical effects of our mind and its worries. The first day of school when your tummy was in knots, or when you were waiting to be told off by your teacher and you needed to rush to the toilet, for example. These symptoms are caused by the very close interplay of mind and body. For some people, this relationship will cause significant symptoms that warrant medical attention.

Our bodies can react very strongly to our mental health and for some people the physical symptoms may be the only sign of anxiety or stress, without any psychological symptoms. Typically patients have said to me 'but I don't feel stressed' – and that is because the body is feeling it rather than the mind. This is called 'somatisation', when our bodies develop physical signs as a result of our mental state, and some physical conditions are more common than others in this scenario.

It can be surprising how disconnected or random these physical symptoms may appear to be. I have a young patient who is incredibly successful, well known in his field, with good self-esteem, who wakes up five or six times a night to pass water. I initiated some tests and investigations as it seemed a pretty dramatic symptom and was really disturbing his sleep, resulting in the knock-on effects of tiredness and poor performance at work. After all the tests came back clear, he asked me if I thought it could be related to anxiety, which surprised me as he is certainly not the personality type one would expect to be feeling anxious and had never disclosed any anxiety to me before. After noting in his diary the nights when it happened over two months, we could see it clearly corresponded to days when work was busy and stressful, but never happened when he was on holiday or at the weekend. A clear link to his mental state was illustrated: a physical bladder issue would not differentiate between Mondays and Saturdays, but a psychological one clearly would.

If you have physical symptoms born from work-related stress or problems, it does not mean those symptoms are not real – they are. Whether a stomach pain comes from anxiety or constipation, you still feel that pain. It is a common misconception to think you are imagining the symptom if it has an emotional cause; that is not the case. The physical symptoms genuinely are there.

Scientific studies show that there are mental aspects to physical diseases and physical aspects to mental ones. When we are scared our hearts race, we sweat, we feel sick and may even have chest pain. This is caused by adrenalin, our fight-or-flight hormone, and increased nervous activity within the brain immediately producing a physical reaction in response to the emotion of fear. However, it is not really known how other mental states cause physical symptoms. What we do know is that when people experience pain in a part of their body they not only have pain nerves firing where the pain is ('peripheral pain'), but also in the brain ('central pain'). This brain involvement mechanism could be central to explaining how tummy aches appear when we are stressed.

Although we don't yet understand the root cause of the relationship between the mind and physical symptoms, there are clear pathways to treating physical conditions where there is likely a strong emotional element. Unsurprisingly this involves addressing any physical issues and ruling out other serious physical conditions, as well as accessing the right psychological help.

The conditions discussed below can also be symptoms of significant physical illnesses, so thorough medical investigation may be necessary. While stress can certainly cause a change in your bowels and abdominal pain, so can cancer, so these physical symptoms all warrant at least a consultation with a doctor. Brushing them off simply as 'stress' is not a good idea until you've had some medical insight.

Getting the right help for these physical conditions will involve acknowledging the issue has emotional and physical aspects, and accepting it is related to your work. This can be the hardest part: many of us can cope with the idea of having headaches from sinusitis, but admitting they are caused by job stress can be difficult, perhaps because it makes us feel weak. There is still a stigma around mental health issues, however minor, and it is almost easier for an individual to accept a physical health issue rather than a mental health one. This often leads patients to search for a physical cause for their symptoms with countless investigations and tests that are not only costly and inconvenient but may actually worsen the problem, increasing anxiety and stress levels – not to mention time off work.

The correct treatment for all of these work-related physical health problems will involve the interplay of the medical treatment as well as psychological and lifestyle help. Even if it is not overt anxiety or depression symptoms you are exhibiting, exploring those in terms of treatment going forward could be very effective. For example, while you would not usually be offered cognitive behavioural therapy, CBT, by a doctor if you are suffering with high blood pressure, it could be discussed as an option if you acknowledge that anxiety from work could be a factor in your physical illness. The psychological treatments may be just as effective in this setting as the pharmaceutical ones.

The most common job-related physical health conditions I see in my practice are outlined below (it is by no means an exhaustive list). My aim is to give you an insight into the symptoms and signs, so that you can recognise these conditions accurately in yourself, and I have explained what the treatment should be, in line with the current medical guidelines. That treatment being not only medication but also the crucial lifestyle changes that are proven to help.

Insomnia

Sleeping trouble is so pervasive and so distressing that while it is really a symptom of other conditions such as depression and anxiety, it deserves its own space. Approximately 15 million prescriptions for sleeping tablets are issued a year in the UK, and that will fall short of the actual number of people suffering who don't go to their doctor or are not given a prescription (as you will see later, sleeping tablets are not actually the correct treatment). Insomnia is incredibly common and it is not surprising that it appears very often as a problem with its origins in the workplace.

Sleeping troubles are a symptom of other conditions including stress, anxiety and depression. There are a wide variety of ways sleep can be affected and insomnia is really considered to be any personal perception that sleep is not enough or effective in terms of quality and quantity. The average adult may need seven hours' sleep a night, but really to have good sleep is to wake up feeling refreshed: no matter how many hours you have slept, if you wake up feeling refreshed you will feel you have slept long enough. Some people, especially as they get older, require only five or six hours to achieve this, while others do need at least the minimum seven hours, if not eight.

When sleep is affected it can be in different ways:

- Not being able to fall asleep

- Waking up repeatedly during the night

- Early morning waking

Different conditions may affect sleep in different ways. For example, depression causes people to wake up very early and prevents them from getting back to sleep. Anxiety often stops people falling asleep at bedtime, as does stress, as people churn over worries in their mind.

The main issue with insomnia is that it makes people feel simply awful. More than one patient has been surprised just how severely insomnia has affected them, urging me to do blood tests and other investigations to look for the cause of how terrible they feel. It has only been when their sleep is corrected and they feel better that they can appreciate just how damaging the insomnia is. Insomnia affects you physically with fatigue, nausea and pain, as well as weakening your immune system in the longer term, making you susceptible to infections. There is scientific evidence that chronic sleep deprivation even increases your risks of diabetes and heart disease due to the effect on your blood pressure and heart rate.

The psychological effects of insomnia, however, are the most crippling and really create the problems. A lack of sleep one night causes you to be jittery, a bit low and irritable the next day. But when that is repeated night after night and week after week, it can have a profound impact on your mental state. Insomnia breeds anxiety and low mood, and worsens feeling stressed and how you cope with these feelings. These problems in turn affect your sleep, worsening the initial problem and a vicious cycle develops. Insomnia thus swiftly impacts your quality of life, affecting your relationships, work and socialising.

If you have insomnia because of your job it can be for many reasons: you might be spending your evenings mulling over issues at work, leaving you unable to switch off at bedtime, or you might find yourself unable to sleep because of the anxiety of what is facing you tomorrow. You simply may be not getting enough sleep due to your hectic routine, early starts and late nights or shift work. (If insomnia is a result of this type of schedule issues, rather than an underlying emotional cause, it will still have the same health consequences.)

Treatment

For years patients and doctors have underestimated the impact – both long- and short-term – of insomnia and just how damaging it can be to someone's health. Even though it is usually a consequence of another issue, it really should warrant its own specific treatment. However, the solution to insomnia is not straightforward.

For decades doctors have issued sleeping tablets, leading to the now huge figures that we prescribe. They were heavily marketed both in the UK and the US and a culture was created with doctors issuing sleeping tablets easily and quickly as a magic bullet. Unfortunately, they are not a quick fix: they do not work for many people and research shows their effects are actually minimal, often creating a quality of sleep that is not optimal. Moreover, they are addictive and cause significant side effects affecting mood, concentration and thought processes. The reliance on them is not unique to patients: doctors depend on them as a swift answer to a very difficult issue that seems hard to fix otherwise. Even though we try not to start long-term courses of sleeping tablets anymore, we do often prescribe short courses to fix a particularly bad period of insomnia and offer immediate relief temporarily.

The correct way to treat insomnia takes time and patience and can seem more taxing than the quick fix of a pill. But these drug-free methods work and improve your sleep long term without the side-effects of sleeping tablets. Ideally insomnia should be treated with the support of a GP or a sleep specialist, as it can involve being referred for psychological therapy as well as treatment of other conditions.

A starting plan of insomnia treatment that you can initiate yourself would involve:

1. **Treat any underlying issues that can impact on your sleep** This will include dealing effectively with anxiety through therapy or dealing with depression with medication or therapy. It would also extend to other issues that are impacting on your sleep, such as pain or needing to wake up to urinate. Find out from your doctor if any tablets you take could be worsening your sleep; an example would be steroids.

2. **Sleep hygiene** This involves creating the perfect environment to encourage and protect sleep. To me it mirrors the very rudimentary approaches parents use to help their children to sleep well, and it is that going back to basics that is effective. It is not considered a cure for insomnia if used alone; however, it is useful to use with other measures. Fundamentally it makes sense to create an environment where you can sleep comfortably so that you are not artificially disturbed: this involves creating the right temperature so that you are not too hot or too cold; removing all light stimulus, including LCD displays on your clock, and perhaps using an eye mask; and reducing any sound disturbances with ear plugs. It is always better to be slightly too cool than too hot, as your body temperature does need to naturally drop slightly as you fall asleep. In essence, you are making yourself as comfortable as you can be, and making the environment as peaceful as it can be.

3. **Bed is only for sex and sleep** You should not be doing anything else in bed. TV, reading and (especially) the smartphone are all meant for elsewhere and should

be done before you get into bed. Your brain needs to re-establish the connection of your bed and sleep, and you need to adopt strict boundaries to do this. Do not plug your phone in by your bed; if you need an alarm, use a simple clock.

4. **Think carefully about what you do in the hours before getting into bed** You should be doing relaxing things like reading or taking a bath, rather than working, exercising or eating. Make sure you eat a long time before going to bed as the changes in blood sugar can act as a stimulus to keep you awake. Likewise avoid caffeine, nicotine and alcohol in the last hours before bed. There is a temptation to have a drink to help you sleep: alcohol may make you tired but in fact it makes sleeping patterns and quality much worse.

5. **Consider eliminating caffeine completely from your diet** This should include not just coffee and tea but cola drinks and chocolate as well. Gradually wean yourself off caffeine over a week or two to avoid any nasty rebound headaches you can get. If you can't come off it completely make caffeine only a choice before lunch, to avoid any of the stimulant effect affecting your sleep.

6. **Exercise** Exercise has a hugely positive effect on sleeping patterns but must be done early in the day, not in the hours before bed. Exercise relaxes the mind, burns energy and is recommended as a goal to implement if you are having difficulty sleeping.

7. **Do not nap** no matter how tired you are. Napping is strictly off limits so that sleep remains only a night-time and in-bed activity.

8. **Fix times to wake up and go to bed and stick to them** This is very important. The idea is to fix the times according to the amount of sleep that you think you need and stick to them rigorously. You have to be realistic about what time you need to be up for work comfortably and set this as the wake-up time, even for weekends. Work backwards to establish a bedtime based on how much sleep you are currently having. Let's say it's six hours to start with and you need to be up for 7 a.m. You should only be going to bed at 1 a.m. Instil this routine, then gradually, once it starts to work, you can bring the bedtime earlier by 15 minutes. This should result in you having consistent nights of solid sleep: it may not be many hours in the first place but it will build up. This is a recognised way of rebuilding a sleeping routine that has become broken.

9. **Put a notepad by your bed** One of the main reasons people cite for not sleeping, particularly in the arena of work-related ill health, is the constant worries going over in their head, or tasks and to-do lists. If you write these down when you think of them, they can be parked and forgotten for the night, so your mind can rest. To encourage your mind to rest even more, saying a non-emotive word over and over again to yourself while in bed can help. A good choice is the word 'the' (known to be better than counting sheep).

10. **Consider going to a sleep clinic** or seeking specific cognitive behavioural therapies via your GP or directly. Such therapies are very effective for sleep and may be offered one on one, online or in a group setting. Techniques may include stimulus-control therapy or sleep restriction therapy. Stimulus-control therapy is a form of CBT focusing on the notion that bed is only

for sleep and sex, with strict instructions to follow on a nightly basis to re-establish the association of bed and sleep. For example, you are taught that if you are in bed and awake for more than 15 minutes, you get out of bed again. It can be incredibly effective. Sleep restriction therapy is a formal way of focusing on the idea laid out in point 8 – cutting the sleep and time in bed right down to the minimum and then gradually building it up, supported with weekly therapy sessions.

High Blood Pressure

High blood pressure is a very common problem affecting over 25 per cent of the adult population in the UK. And it is also a very significant one: no matter what the cause, it is known to be a substantial risk factor for heart diseases including heart attacks and angina, stroke and kidney disease. All of these diseases are life-changing and can also be life-threatening. In the context of work-related illness high blood pressure is a very major condition to have, if it is a result of your job.

For many people we do not know why they get high blood pressure – we call this 'essential hypertension'. However, it is well known that high blood pressure is associated with other problems, such as diabetes, and is more likely in certain situations, such as when you have a family history of the condition or with increasing age. It is seen more commonly in people who have a lot of stress but also who have a lifestyle that may come about through increased stress, such as a lack of exercise, poor sleep, high caffeine intake or drinking too much alcohol. So both the stress and your lifestyle that results from stress can cause high blood pressure. There is no doubt that work-related problems can cause and exacerbate high blood pressure and it is an issue I have seen recurrently over the last ten years, across the range of work-based issues.

The physical responses to emotional stress are triggered by the fight-or-flight hormones adrenalin and cortisol. In the first instance, they increase your heart rate and blood pressure so you are ready literally to run or fight. This is an essential physiological state and works well. What doesn't work well is when that stress response, and therefore physiological response, are repeated over and over, leaving you in a persistently heightened state of stress. This will keep your blood pressure at higher levels for longer periods of time, as those fighting hormones race around your bloodstream: essentially you then have a diagnosis of high blood pressure as your blood pressure is up more often than down.

Blood pressure is always quoted using two figures; the first is the systolic measurement, when your heart is contracting and pumping blood around your body, and the second – the diastolic – when it is relaxed. This gives readings that should look something like 120/80 in a normal reading for example. High blood pressure or hypertension is considered to be regular, consistent readings over 140/90 when taken with a healthcare professional, or 135/85 when taken at home (when you are assumed to be more relaxed!).

Symptoms

For the majority of sufferers, high blood pressure will not display symptoms and therefore it is usually diagnosed incidentally on a health check or during an examination for another reason. Some people feel they experience certain headaches or eye symptoms with higher blood pressure, but most people will not know. Doctors will only diagnose the condition on a series of readings and usually with measurements taken at home – because of the strong link between stress and blood pressure, it is thought that simply being with a healthcare professional raises your blood pressure so giving an artificially high reading. As a result of acknowledging this association, doctors will now use home testing for blood pressure. You may be advised to buy a home testing machine or be given a blood pressure measurement device to wear for 24 hours. The aim of this is to see how your blood pressure varies throughout the day and your ordinary life, but fundamentally to see if your average blood pressure is high enough for treatment. The results can make particularly interesting reading if you are suffering as a result of your work and the pattern can be clear to see.

Treatment

Without a doubt high blood pressure requires treatment in order to reduce your risks of the life-threatening and life-changing illnesses it can cause. That treatment is as much about lifestyle as it is about medications, although medications tend to be prescribed swiftly.

Medication for high blood pressure follows strict guidelines and will be chosen by your GP according to your age, kidney function and other conditions you may have. Commonly, people are started on tablets such as ramipril, losartan or amlodipine, but these may be changed and increased as your response is monitored.

Hypertension is usually treated with medication because of the pressing need to get the numbers better, quickly, and so reduce long-term health risks. But there are firm guidelines from the established medical bodies to look at lifestyle changes as part of the overall management of the condition. Specifically for high blood pressure, attention needs to be paid to reducing caffeine intake, alcohol intake and salt to a level lower than 6g a day.

Adopting planned lifestyle changes where you improve sleep and exercise levels will help your blood pressure. The mainstay of what you need to do for yourself is to reduce or ameliorate the issues that have resulted in your work problems, reducing your stress and improving how you feel mentally. Fostering these through the steps outlined in chapters 5 and 6 will reduce your work-induced stress and therefore improve your high blood pressure. Doctors recognise that while we cannot prescribe relaxation therapy for patients, options such as stress management techniques, active relaxation and meditation or mindfulness can all help to improve blood pressure, particularly when there is a known environmental cause. Treating high blood pressure successfully will be as much about what you can do for yourself, as what your doctor can prescribe.

Irritable Bowel Syndrome

From childhood we notice how closely our gut is related to nerves, anxiety and stress. When we feel nervous and we can't eat breakfast; when we have butterflies in our stomach before a big test; when we need to rush to the loo because we are afraid. For a long time there has been a known association between how our minds are feeling and how under pressure we are, and how our digestive system reacts. It is no surprise therefore that work stress and job issues can cause digestive problems.

It is an old wives tale, although still quoted even in doctors' surgeries, that stress causes stomach ulcers. In fact it has been shown to be most unlikely that stomach ulcers are caused by stress; however, there is certainly a common link between life stress and all types of emotional turmoil and other digestive issues, notably irritable bowel syndrome (IBS).

It is not totally clear how stress causes IBS but studies have shown a high correlation of the condition with a diagnosis of anxiety. Some estimates show that if you look at patients with IBS, over half will have symptoms to fulfil the criteria for a mental health condition – usually anxiety but also depression and stress disorders. The chemical or physiological link has not been definitively identified but there are certain theories behind this:

- Anxiety doesn't cause IBS but people with IBS are more sensitive to emotional turmoil such as stress and anxiety.

- Although it doesn't cause IBS, anxiety and stress will trigger symptoms in those with the condition: around half of patients in an IBS clinic attribute the onset of their symptoms to a stressful event.

- Stress and anxiety worsen negative feelings including pain and may heighten the awareness of spasms and pain within the gut.

- IBS may be triggered by the immune system, which we know is weakened by stress.

- Stress appears to increase the amount of inflammation within the body, which may be a part of the process.

Symptoms

IBS is a digestive condition that is usually chronic (long-lasting) and comes and goes in episodes affecting how the digestive system works. Unlike other bowel and gut diseases the characteristic features of the disease are that all investigation results are normal: there are no structural changes or blood tests that are found to be abnormal. In order to be diagnosed with IBS you therefore need to experience the clear set of symptoms that define the disease:

- Abdominal pain that is changed for the better or worse by opening your bowels

- Disruption of your bowel habit – so either diarrhoea, constipation or both

- Abdominal bloating

Although you may not realise (generally people don't discuss their bowels so openly), it is in fact a very common condition, likely affecting as many as 20 per cent of UK adults. Most usually it affects people between the ages of twenty and thirty, and is twice as common in women as in men. It is hard to say how long people will be affected and for some it will be a lifelong condition. Interestingly, in terms of job-related health, one study looking at the prognosis in those with IBS showed that ongoing life stress prolongs the illness and hinders your recovery (reason enough to start sorting your work issues out!). Comparing IBS patients both with and without stress, none of those with ongoing life stress recovered after 16 months, compared with 41 per cent of those without stress, who did.

Because of the strong association between the gut and the mind, anyone can experience episodes of IBS-like symptoms in the short term – before a job interview for example, or during a particularly bad week. Therefore to make the diagnosis, you really need to have had symptoms consistently for more than six months. As there are no formal blood tests or diagnostic investigations, your symptom history is crucial. An accurate diary of your symptoms can prove very valuable in the diagnosis: you will need to show the pattern of the stereotypical symptoms, as well as other symptoms including fatigue, nausea, headaches and even bladder symptoms. While there are no blood tests to confirm the diagnosis, they will often be done to rule out other bowel diseases and this is vital. IBS is very common compared to bowel cancer but they can mimic one another; as a doctor, it is very important to contemplate the other, more serious diagnosis, which must not be missed, before settling on a conclusive diagnosis.

Treatment

In the guidelines for treating IBS in the UK, the first line advises doctors to encourage their patients to identify their sources of stress and explore ways to relax. If you are suffering with IBS because of your work or job, then it is clear from the scientific evidence that dealing with that issue is the essential foundation of your treatment. Exploring all the lifestyle changes and job adaptations discussed in chapters 5 and 6 will directly affect your symptoms. Any way to relieve the issues with your job, whether through active relaxation and stress management or directly dealing with the problems you face in the workplace, will reduce emotional upset and thereby improve your symptoms.

Other than reducing stress, lifestyle treatments for IBS specifically focus on diet and exercise. Being a digestive disorder means of course diet has a role to play, and, specifically, sufferers of IBS need to:

- look at their intake of insoluble fibre, e.g., bran, which may need reducing, and increase levels of soluble fibre such as oats

- explore the FODMAP diet – where the amounts of fermentable sugars, which cause bloating, in certain fruit and vegetables are reduced (see Resources, page 217, for more information)

- add oats and linseeds to reduce bloating

- avoid starchy processed foods that often sit undigested in the colon

- consider cutting out wheat or dairy foods for a while to see if that improves your symptoms

- consider taking a probiotic

Specifically, consider if your work and your dietary habits around work are contributing to your IBS symptoms. In other words, think about not just the stress or problems with work but also the practicalities of what you eat and how you eat during a working week. More than one of my patients has symptoms worsened by what is available to eat in the work canteen and has changed their routine accordingly, opting for a packed lunch (more time-consuming but less pain). If you have IBS, grabbing a processed breakfast or wolfing down a sandwich at your desk will not help the way you feel.

Exercise is important for IBS, both in terms of improving your food's transit time within the gut and also in the stress relief and mood uplift it brings.

Doctors prescribe various medications for IBS but these do not offer a cure for the condition, they merely help to manage the symptoms of bloating, constipation, diarrhoea and pain. That is why the lifestyle changes and the self-help is so important: there is no alternative quick fix.

Psychological therapies specifically for IBS can focus on anxiety and stress directly in order to improve the severity and frequency of your symptoms. It is worth investigating those available to you (see Chapter 5) to directly improve your mental state and therefore your IBS.

Headaches

The tension headache is well known to many of us but regular headaches day in, day out can be very distressing. Headaches themselves are common, particularly in relation to stress; but they are also easily precipitated by the workplace environment – hours staring at a computer screen, stuffy offices, poor posture at a desk, caffeine intake and erratic eating patterns will all contribute even if someone has no stress from their job. So it is easy to understand why headaches are a common manifestation of work-related ill health.

Tension headaches occur on both sides of the head and feel like a band of stress pressing or tightening around the head. People can feel pressure behind the eyes and a tightening of their neck muscles. These symptoms are important to clarify with headaches: they are very different from the headache people get with migraine, and that difference is key for treatment and prognosis. A tension headache can last for anything from half an hour to a week. You would be considered to have chronic tension headaches if you were suffering for more than half the days in a month – it is thought that up to 3 per cent of adults in the UK are in this position.

With any emotional upset the perception of pain can be heightened and intensified – we see that all pain conditions are associated, triggered and exacerbated by our mental state. The exact reason why people get headaches specifically is not known, but it is possibly related to an increase in muscular activity within the scalp. This could be the result of muscles tensing through stress or stress increasing muscle inflammation. As well as stress, tension headaches can also be triggered by a lack of sleep.

Whatever the possible cause, headaches are a very important symptom to assess and define correctly. Migraine is also an incredibly common diagnosis and some schools of thought believe many people are told that they have tension headaches when in fact they suffer from migraine. Very rarely are chronic headaches the sign of anything sinister, but it is crucial to have that possibility explored. This is one area where keeping a diary of your symptoms (see page 93) is going to be incredibly useful to assess the frequency and severity of the headaches you get, as well as the symptoms and possible triggers such as eating, stress and posture. Any chronic headache should be discussed with a GP for a full assessment.

Unsurprisingly, the treatment of tension headaches aims to relieve the tension. The medical treatment of the condition involves using the right pain relief for you that will allow you to function without side effects, avoid addiction and manage day to day without the pain and distress that ensues.

But primarily managing the chronic headaches of tension and stress involve the removal – or at least the reduction – of that stress. As well as dealing with the stress, it is also important to remove any physical issues that may be adding to your headaches. Even if these are not the primary cause of your headaches, improving these could at least lessen the problem, so it's very much worth a try. Consider specifically whether you can improve the following known headache triggers:

- Your posture at work and the effect this has on your neck muscles

- Your eating habits

- Your caffeine intake

- Your screen usage

- Your water intake

Recurrent Illness

It is very common for a consultation to start with the words 'I feel like I am ill all the time', with patients convinced that they pick up whatever bug is going around the office, and even when no one else seems to be ill, they fall sick with some sort of virus or infection.

Usually I can see the impetus for coming to the doctor is more out of concern that a serious disease is attacking the immune system, as well as trying to solve what is incredibly inconvenient and draining. For someone who is busy with work, or weighed down by issues from a job, being constantly struck down with coughs and colds is very distressing. Having to be off work with flu or missing crucial deadlines and meetings only adds to stress; likewise if you are struggling with a boss or a colleague, doing so when you are feeling below par or having to ask for sick leave often inflames the situation. While the illnesses themselves tend not to be serious, the effect on quality of life and how you feel day to day can be. And it is also, understandably, a source of worry.

As well as causing stress and worry, recurrent illness can also be the result of any stress and worry you are feeling at work. Stress and emotional issues are well known to knock the immune system, weakening its fight against common infections. Combine that with poor sleep, poor eating habits and little time to exercise or relax and the situation is even worse. Many people going to work will also be in contact with a plethora of germs thanks to public transport or a jam-packed workplace – this doesn't help the situation!

Stress will make people vulnerable to coughs, colds, flu and the other infections that frequently circulate. It can equally cause the appearance and recurrence of other less common infections such as shingles, herpes cold sores, thrush and even pneumonia.

Generally if you are suffering with 'simple' viral infections like coughs and colds that resolve completely and naturally in their own time, then this is not a worry medically. Such a scenario would not be a red flag to look for an underlying physical health issue or weakness in your immune system. It is more of a concern if you are getting more unusual infections, very serious ones or you are not able to fight the illnesses naturally; this would be the time to investigate the immune system and explore what else could be the underlying cause.

If you are suffering with recurrent illnesses, ensure you keep a good record of what is going on and what symptoms you have. When you feel rough and stressed out with work and illness together, it is hard to keep track in your mind and remember accurately details and symptoms. We all have a tendency to overplay worries when we are stressed, and even catastrophising, so it can be really helpful – for you and your doctor – to keep a record over a three-month period of what is actually going on. Keeping some sort of record or diary is an important part of planning a recovery from work-related ill health (see Chapter 4).

Treatment

It is absolutely worth speaking to a doctor if you feel you are ill all the time. You need the medical assessment of the severity of the infections and opinion on whether or not further investigations are warranted. Of course, you may also need medical treatment for any infections, and your doctor may consider it worth you seeking preventative measures such as immunisations against shingles or flu for example.

Treating and preventing recurrent illnesses very much involves looking at the root causes of your stress and tackling the work-related problems you are facing: if stress is causing this issue, then tackling that stress needs to be the mainstay of your treatment. This type of scenario where you are ill all the time responds very well to the action plan of Chapter 6 – particularly in terms of sleep, diet and exercise, all of which are known to directly help the immune system. To recover from viruses and other infections, you need time and rest and some self-TLC. And you need the same to prevent the problems from happening in the first instance. Improving your work–life balance and your lifestyle, and helping yourself with a recovery plan should stop you being ill so often.

Specifically, to fight infections and boost your immune system you can look at taking vitamin supplements. Although vitamins should not be taken as a substitute for a poor diet, it can be a good idea to take them to correct any potential, even small, deficiencies that could contribute to a weakened immune system. There is no need to take mega-doses of individual vitamins or spend a small fortune in a health food shop, but taking a daily multivitamin tablet can be an easy, simple part of a broader plan to make you feel better. The immune system requires vitamins C, D and E, selenium and zinc; any supplement you look at should include a full complement of each of those for it to be worthwhile.

Worsening Chronic Conditions

If you are already suffering with a physical health problem, then any stress or emotional turmoil can worsen it. This is particularly the case for chronic skin conditions such as psoriasis, eczema and rosacea where it is fully recognised that stress is a trigger. We also see stress as an exacerbating factor in a range of pain conditions such as arthritis, endometriosis and back pain, and even in chronic physical illnesses such as heart disease and diabetes.

If you are dealing with a condition that waxes and wanes, you will expect to have episodes where you feel OK or even good and episodes where you are suffering more. It is common to see the worse episodes when you are experiencing periods of stress or chronic stress, which can occur when work is a problem.

Many of the chronic conditions are related to inflammation within the body; psoriasis, for example, is an inflammatory skin condition, where the immune system has turned on the body and inflammation is in overdrive. Likewise with many types of arthritis. Inflammation is supposed to be one of the body's protective reactions, in response to injury or infection, but in many chronic conditions it is actually too much inflammation that causes the problem. Research indicates that stress affects both the immune system and the amount of inflammation, and so these conditions can worsen. Coupled with the fact that living and working with a chronic condition is stressful in itself, it is easy to see how a downward spiral is created.

Pain conditions are inextricably linked to stress and emotional tension. When we are stressed and worried, muscles tense and contract for extended periods of time, perpetuating aches and pains that already exist. Our perception of pain is also heightened.

The routine of your work, or your workplace itself, can also add to the issues faced with a chronic condition – not being able to apply treatments in privacy for example, difficulties timing medication with food breaks, or not being given the freedom to move or exercise as you need with an arthritis condition. These are not work-caused job illnesses, but they are worsened as a result of the work setting and work pattern.

It would be remiss of me not to mention back pain here and other joint and muscular pains in relation to work-related ill health, given they account for 8.8 million working days lost each year in the UK. Work-related musculoskeletal conditions are incredibly common, accounting for 41 per cent of all job-related ill health according to statistics from the Health and Safety Executive. These issues are often not pre-existing chronic conditions but originate from the job setting and physical activities that come with it – your body position, repetitive movements and long hours. However, it is recognised that musculoskeletal problems, including back pain, are affected and worsened by psychosocial issues at work such as relationships, your work timetable and the prevailing culture or problems set out in Chapter 1. It is usually a combination of influences that causes these problems to persist. Over 3 million working days are lost each year due to back pain alone; we know that stress worsens any pain or perception of pain, and experts believe – particularly with back pain – that the emotional factors at work have as much of a role to play as the physical ones.

All pain and inflammatory conditions will respond well to the active, lifestyle approaches this book focuses on in Chapters 5 and 6. With a chronic condition it is vital to get the appropriate medical help as the foundation of treatment, while adding in your own lifestyle measures. With the help of the appropriate people (see Chapter 5) it is critical to work out what adaptations at work will help and improve your condition. These adaptations should be formally adopted, preferably with help from occupational health specialists but perhaps also with a Fitness to Work statement, which your GP can write.

Work-related stress can cause a variety of physical health ailments which may appear alone or in combination with mental health symptoms. It may be hard initially to realise or accept these are related to your job, but now you can see that it is vital for you to acknowledge that physical symptoms do not only originate from physical problems. Our minds and bodies are inextricably linked and stress on the mind will often cause stress on the body, and vice versa. The crucial part of recovery for any of these issues is to recognise the true cause, and appreciate that psychological and lifestyle changes are as fundamental to treatment as medication.

Now you understand your health condition you can go on to build your recovery.

CHAPTER 4

•

Facing the Problem

We have seen how it is possible for your job to make you ill, and what your illness will most likely look like. Having explored specific treatment options for your condition, the subsequent chapters set out a structured recovery strategy for anyone who has a job-related illness. This encompasses the following processes (explored over the next few chapters):

- Acknowledging the problem

- Seeking the right help and advice from the right people

- Improving your life and fostering a recovery while you continue your job

- Taking time away from work

From the earlier chapters outlining symptoms and causes for job-related illness, you have now established there could be an issue with your work affecting your health; how you take the next steps is very important for protecting your health and also your career and income.

This can feel like a frightening, confusing and stigmatising position to be in and it can be difficult to know what to do for the best. Theoretically, it is easy just to call it quits and jump ship, leaving the job that is the source of your illness. In reality of course, few people would ever be able to take this option; aside from the financial side of things, you have to safeguard your ongoing career progression and CV, your self-esteem and often your standing within your profession, or even within your community and social circle.

So the first time you find yourself thinking your job could be making you ill can be a whirlwind. This is even more dramatic if you are suffering with a mental health condition such as stress or anxiety, as that makes clear thinking very hard indeed. For anyone, at any level of seniority, it can be very challenging to think rationally and lucidly when faced with the notion that your job has effectively 'gone wrong'. The whole issue plays into personal feelings of failure, guilt and worries about your future and your family's well-being. While all these feelings are totally understandable, natural and unavoidable, they can stand in the way of your dealing well with the situation and affording yourself the optimal plan of action.

Having a concrete, step-by-step idea of what to do next can give you some structure in what can be a particularly structure-less situation. How you adopt this plan will be different for each individual, but the basic steps of acknowledgement, seeking help and adopting change all amount to the same solution and a better path into the future. This all has to be forged while protecting your job, your finances and your self-esteem. The idea is not a 'one-size fits all'. How an individual reacts to work-related illness depends of course on so many factors, but there are multiple areas in which anyone in any job can look for solutions.

Ensuring you are looking after yourself personally maintains your mental and physical health enough to see you through the process. That is why in the following plan of what to do, diet and mindfulness play a role alongside formal employment processes. Concentrating on lifestyle changes and your well-being can very much help you through this testing time, even if you feel poorly motivated to do so. It may be that you cannot alter the big problems with work, but you should be able to build up your physical and mental strength and resilience to help you cope with those challenges.

In practice, the people I have seen who have survived and thrived through a work health crisis have done so by following the notion that these more trivial details, or *micro-actions*, are as vital as the big-deal ones. Even if you are going to change your career, go for redundancy or fight a grievance battle, it shouldn't stop you concentrating on smaller, everyday moves to protect your mind and health. That all adds to your own personal strength and will improve any outcomes. You can lose that all-important sense of achievement with job loss or failure, and this can fuel a downward spiral. Fostering tiny successes through micro-actions away from your work helps to lessen the negative feelings and aids a recovery.

Planning a recovery starts with acknowledging the issue – a process you effectively initiated when you picked up this book. This may well be the trickiest part of all, as the fundamental idea of accepting you have a problem can be emotionally hard. This may be the first time in your life you have been ill, the first time you think you have a mental health issue, and naturally it is a massive dent to your pride as well as terribly disappointing. I would say everyone I have looked after in this situation has suffered these emotions, and they can be pretty upsetting and tough to deal with.

The process begins with acceptance and affirmation as its foundation so you can start to foster your recovery and wellness, and – hopefully – effect change within your working life. Acceptance is necessary to focus on positive changes and forge a plan that will be sustainable. We are now working towards an incredibly solution-focused approach with a clear goal: to improve your health. It is unlikely you will have a healthcare professional or work mentor who can structure this for you; it all relies on you, focusing on your working life, career ladder, family needs and health needs to create a plan that is realistic and suitable for your situation.

The following chapters are designed to give you back a level of control and empowerment. Your recovery starts now.

Acknowledging You Have an Issue

You need to acknowledge the problem: this is the critical first step. You really have to be honest with yourself. At this stage you are not making any decisions about whether you are going to resign, change jobs, take time off or plan anything dramatic. This is simply the start of the process. You will isolate and define the issue, and start what will be a step-by-step process to improve the situation and therefore your health. You have already initiated the process by buying this book and exploring the causes and conditions described in the earlier chapters. This has been the subconscious initial stage of admitting you have an issue.

The steps to acknowledging work-related ill health are:

1. Keep a record of your symptoms and how you feel

2. Be honest with yourself

3. Lose the stigma

4. Talk to family and friends

5. Start a plan of action

Step 1: Keep a diary of how you feel

Symptom diaries are now commonly used in medicine in order to ascertain symptom patterns, causes and the natural history of any illness. They can be a very useful diagnostic tool and give a tremendous amount of clear information in a very simple way.

Doctors often use symptom diaries to diagnose migraine and irritable bowel syndrome, as well as psychosomatic and environmentally induced conditions. They are absolutely invaluable if you are concerned that your work is making you ill. I would recommend starting a diary as a first step for anyone feeling they are suffering from their job, no matter what the circumstances. Even if you are absolutely certain the job is the issue and you have no problem accepting or acknowledging that, a symptom diary still has a lot of value at the start of the process of recovery – and it's very straight-forward to keep.

Over the years in general practice I have seen how easy it is to get the particulars wrong with our memory of personal experience and personal symptoms. Far too often we look back at symptoms we have and wrongly remember how severe they were, or when exactly they happened and specifically how many episodes there were. It is very normal in clinic for me to hear a patient say 'I came to see you about my leg a couple of months ago', while with the computerised records in front of me I am able to point out it was over a year ago. With busy lives and lots going on it is not easy to remember and isolate the specifics accurately. It is especially hard if you are feeling unwell mentally or physically, both of which can make brains foggy and memories vaguer.

It is also tricky to be specific about the details if your symptoms are equivocal, intermittent or have come on gradually. Was it actually a Wednesday after the weekly meetings that you got those headaches? Was it every Wednesday or were some in fact OK? Do you really always feel better on a Sunday or is that how you remember it, because we all expect to feel good on a Sunday? Our memories are not always as accurate as we think they are, particularly if we have repeatedly talked over an issue, worried about it or subconsciously given it undue momentum and significance. Likewise many personality types are inclined to underplay symptoms and how often they happen. The beauty of noting symptoms, dates and situations in a diary is that it creates an artificial and accurate memory, uninfluenced by our perceptions, and therefore aids an accurate diagnosis.

The diary serves a vital function beyond just diagnosing the problem. It is very useful to have the objective evidence of what is going on in black and white as part of your acknowledgement of the situation. This will undoubtedly help to cement in your mind the notion that there is an issue which, as we have said, can be very hard. Acknowledgement is tricky and awkward, especially when you may not want to see it, and having that specific and qualitative detail can really help you accept what is going on. It is hard to argue with a timetable that clearly indicates your palpitations only happen Monday to Friday.

Additionally, it may also be useful to have your symptom diary as objective evidence going forward. Even with the best-laid plans, in the best working environments and with your best intentions, things can go wrong. It is possible you may find yourself in a situation of needing to apply for sick leave or needing to leave work completely. You may even be subject at some stage to formal employment proceedings, and having detailed evidence of what has been happening can be really beneficial. The chances are you won't need it but I have certainly seen cases where, sadly, this type of substantiation has been necessary. To a third party, a detailed list of dates and symptoms is far more credible than a simple subjective statement such as *the job was giving me headaches*. So it is worth having this just as a very simple and straightforward safety net.

A useful symptom diary would ideally cover at least one month, although six weeks would be good, and if you can stick at it for two months even better. It can sometimes take that long to see the pattern, especially if problematic situations happen less frequently and symptoms are more intermittent or varied. Sometimes a pattern is so crystal clear after a month that you don't need any more evidence.

The following details should be included in your diary:

- The date and time

- The situation: this can be as simple as 'work' or 'meeting' or 'day off'

- The symptoms you felt and the severity of those symptoms

I would also strongly recommend writing 'no symptoms' each day this applies, so that when you look back you know specifically you had no symptoms rather than just you forgot to write something. That way you can get in the habit of writing something every day but also be confident your diary is an accurate record. Set yourself a prompt on your phone each day to remind yourself to document something.

The idea is not to have a Brontë-style journal of your life at work, but a non-emotional, quantitative description of what is going on chronologically. It needs to be detailed enough to be worthwhile, but quick to do and not over-complicated. A simple example is given below.

Monday	Tuesday	Wednesday	Thursday	Friday	Saturday	Sunday
Work	Work	Work	Work	Day off		
		Worked late to prep for meeting – left at 9 p.m.	Budget meeting with Steve			
Headache – mild, didn't take anything	Headache – moderate, needed tablets	No symptoms	No symptoms	Headache before bed, didn't take anything	Felt good	Slight headache in the evening

Over the years in general practice, I have found this an invaluable way of measuring and detecting a range of issues, particularly when it comes to work-related ill health. It is amazing the number of times I have shown patients their symptoms occur Monday to Friday, or only on the days when 'that' colleague is in. Likewise, we can sometimes show that in fact a patient's symptoms are not situational but occur just as often at the weekends and on holiday as at work.

Step 2: Be honest with yourself

With the black-and-white evidence in front of you, you now have to accept and admit that there is an issue and it needs dealing with. If your job is indeed making you ill, you need to accept this and be honest with yourself in order to forge a path to recovery.

Admitting there is an issue is something that has to come from you and it has to surpass all those feelings of guilt, failure, disappointment and apprehension about the future. These are enormous emotions to face and it can be distressing to feel like this. However, acknowledgement and facing these distressing emotions will truly help you to structure a recovery that is suited to you and your physical and psychological needs.

Acceptance is a recognised psychological or emotional state. It does not mean you are weak or that you just willingly submit to the tricky situation you find yourself in. In fact, it is the opposite: you can accept and face up to the fact that your job is making you ill and look to change that reality. Fighting the issue, ignoring it and not facing up to its existence will only lead to more inner turmoil and angst, as you struggle against additional negative feelings on top of your work-related symptoms.

In psychological terms, acceptance of an issue comes at the start of the process to resolve things: it is the springboard to change and recovery.

Step 3: Lose the stigma

There really should be no stigma relating to any health problem, but sadly there still is, even in a forward-thinking and liberal society. The 'sick role' brings with it a certain feeling of weakness within us, even when we can rationalise that it is out of our control. Unwittingly we see others with ill health as being weaker or less capable, and this societal view reinforces the stigma that accompanies illness.

Suffering from work-related ill health is no more a sign of weakness or underachievement than suffering from any other ailment. It is just that no one really talks about it freely and readily. Because our self-esteem and status are tied up with our work, it is not a comfortable issue to admit so remains hugely stigmatised.

As a GP I can see that if you suffer from work-related illness you are absolutely not alone. The whole motivation for this book was the sheer number of people I see in your position and the vast range of people affected, from the top to the bottom of the employment hierarchy. I have seen a huge array of job-related physical illnesses and psychological conditions in people who just don't know where to turn or who didn't even realise their job was to blame. And I suspect that is the tip of the iceberg. For every one consulting their GP, there are almost certainly thousands of others seeking help and guidance elsewhere. There are many workers muddling through alone or continuing to suffer, and plenty more who don't even realise how much work is affecting them.

I have seen work-related ill health affect people across the spectrum, from the most capable, highest achievers to the happiest, unflappable and most diligent employees, and across all ages and genders. It isn't something you can predict happening and should not have any stigma associated with it. Indeed, as we have seen, for every 100,000 people going to work, on average 1,230 will have job-related stress and in some industries the figure will be much higher. That figure will also fall short of the real number as these are only those people who are formally diagnosed or recorded through government or healthcare statistics. There really shouldn't be any shame in such a widespread issue.

(It is also worth you knowing that over the months I was writing this book, when friends and acquaintances asked what the title was, the most common response I heard was: 'I could be one of your case-studies!')

As an idea, in order to quash that stigma, here is a small sample of the list of occupations of those patients I have seen in clinic with work-related ill health:

- Taxi drivers

- Teachers

- Doctors

- Nurses

- Retail workers

- Civil servants

- Laboratory technicians

- Accountants

- Corporate lawyers

- Self-employed business people

- Journalists

- Television and radio production staff

- Beauticians

- Secretaries

- Actors and performers

- Childcare workers

- Builders

- Train drivers

Why certain people will fall ill because of their job stress and others won't is hard to quantify. I am also not sure if it is hugely valuable to ask, 'Why did this happen?', the answer to which you can't change, rather than, 'What can I do now?' The answer to *this* question is very much now in your control.

Psychologists tend to talk about *resilience*: our emotional resilience is a protective strength that allows people to cope with and get over stress, hardships and adversities both physical and emotional. It gives us the power to carry on, move on and overcome whatever is thrown at us and to adapt, rather than succumbing. Building resilience happens from childhood and is fostered throughout our lives, but some is naturally inherent within our personalities and our genes. Resilience will play a part in who will and won't suffer with work-related illness, and some people will of course be more resilient to the stresses and problems within a working environment. But it is certainly not the complete picture, as much will depend on circumstances, the specific issues and the personalities involved. I have seen many 'resilient' patients who have coped with life traumas and prior troubles, who then sadly suffer with work-related illness: I don't think one can predict who is going to be affected and always explain why it happens.

Step 4: Talk to family and friends

Talking to friends and family might seem like a trivial activity, but in fact it can offer some really important fundamentals of your recovery, namely:

- Acceptance

- Support

- Advice

Once you have acknowledged and admitted your work-related illness to yourself, the next step in the process of acceptance is to start to talk about it with your family and friends. This fosters support and affirmation and underpins a successful start to a recovery.

Talking to people who love you and care about you achieves a huge amount emotionally. It may feel like a huge hurdle but it is an essential one to start the next stage of the process. Your family and friends are usually the least judgemental and most forgiving people in your life, who respect you as a partner, a friend, a sibling rather than defining you by the job you do – so these are the people to start with.

Take an opportunity, when you have plenty of time and space to say what you think is going on, and start the conversation. These initial conversations can give you huge perspective, as insights gained will be from people who are close enough to you to see the signs, but just far enough removed to have more objectivity and less emotion.

While you might think that you are a bit stressed from work and feel it is becoming a problem, in fact what your partner sees is someone totally unmotivated and burnt out, and they can't believe you've not mentioned it before now. Or it might be that they notice a stark difference between the way you behave during the week and the weekend, or since you started your current job. Conversely, they might tell you that actually your symptoms started long before your distressing work situation, for example, and in fact you need to look beyond that as a cause. Sometimes, once you raise the subject, it will allow them to broach what they feel is the issue, or mention different symptoms that you may not be acutely aware of but which are just as significant.

You certainly don't need to speak to many people; the aim is simply to open up a conversation with those closest to you for the purpose of affirmation and support. One conversation could be enough.

If you are going to discuss work-related ill health, then talking to people at work is going to be tricky. Many people make their closest friends at work, which is understandable when you spend eight hours a day together, week in, week out. Going through the successes and failures of work, and the ups and downs of personal life with colleagues of course cultivates close friendships within the working environment. But if you think something about your job or working environment is making you ill, then discussing it with work friends is going to blur lines and complicate the matter. You don't want to compromise colleagues, start a mutiny, change any battlelines or unwittingly put co-workers in a position where they feel they have to take a side or make a stand. I think it is essential to separate these first conversations entirely from your job: this process is for you now and it needs to be initiated away from work.

A huge benefit to these initial conversations is the psychological support and encouragement that can come from the notion of 'me too'. Work illness and stress is so common that the chances are someone close to you has been through something similar, or is aware of someone else who has gone through something similar. It is incredibly helpful to hear that someone you know has experienced the same sort of thing, especially if they have come out the other side and can offer some advice and guidance as an added bonus. This reduces the stigma and makes you feel more normal despite the distressing situation – the emotional support of 'me too' can he hugely valuable.

Advice from friends and family comes in all forms, and you have to accept that some of it will be entirely useless practically but great emotionally, or vice versa. You also have to be prepared for the unwarranted advice and learn to filter it – this is a danger of opening up to many people, some of whom may offer advice you don't want or don't need, or that is actually damaging! But support, advice and acceptance from friends and family is invaluable, and sometimes the smallest piece of advice may in fact prove to be a gem, as happened in this case:

Case Study

An associate of mine was made redundant from his well-paid corporate job and suddenly found himself urgently looking for work. In fact his job had been causing him huge amounts of stress, working in a toxic environment under a despotic yet ineffectual boss. But while it was a good thing to be out of that environment, it was still incredibly distressing for him to lose his job so suddenly with no planning. Although recovery was important, finding a job and an income quickly was the most urgent matter. When you are used to the routine of your job, it can be very difficult to structure a day or a week when you aren't working, but he was diligent about meeting potential employers, recruitment consultants and (to be honest) any acquaintance or ex-colleague who could offer a lead in terms of work. He had a full timetable of weekly meetings focused on networking and securing a job quickly. But often between those meetings he had an hour or two to spare when he just wanted to find somewhere to sit, use his laptop and prepare for his next meeting. He found himself spending five or ten pounds each day buying coffee just so he could sit in a coffee shop, think and use the WiFi – not the ideal scenario when you have just lost your salary.

A few weeks into his new schedule he was at a party, talking to a friend, and the topic of work came up. He opened up about what had happened and how he was trying to get himself sorted. It turned out his friend had been in the same boat a few years earlier, and had a very similar period of time engaging in meetings and ▶

networking trying to find work. And then he offered him the most surprising and unexpected advice for what to do in between meetings: 'You walk into a café and do what you would never do – sit at the dirty table. Sit where the used cups and plates are, the waiters think you have already eaten and won't bother you.' Free seat, free WiFi and the in-between meeting stop-overs were solved.

That was a great tip, but there was also the tremendous power of 'me too' – hearing someone say they had been in the same situation. No matter how successful you have been, these things can happen to everyone and there is no shame. Even if you need to sit down with someone else's dirty cups.

Step 5: Start your plan of action

This chapter has dealt with a hard process: recognising and admitting there is a problem. This may come about organically, but the steps in this chapter have provided a structure to enable you to do this properly and definitively. Through recognising there could be an issue and keeping your symptom diary, and through initial conversations with family and friends, you have firmly acknowledged and faced the problem of your work-related ill health. Along with an understanding of your illness and the problems with your job, you have an excellent foundation for the next stage of your recovery – seeking the help you need.

Now it is time to look to the practical next steps, plan what is going to work for you and build your recovery. In the next two chapters you will establish who can help you and how, and how you can help yourself.

CHAPTER 5

•

Who Can Help You?

When you first establish you are ill as a result of your job, it is all too easy to get no help and feel adrift, or to find too much and be completely overwhelmed. It is common to seek advice and counsel far and wide but end up with nothing useful. Likewise, it is easy to bury your head in the sand and not feel able to confront the situation head-on by asking for help. When you are unwell, while both extremes are totally understandable, neither is at all helpful. To help you avoid either scenario, this chapter will set out whose advice is worth seeking in the first instance to really focus your discussions and efforts to recover.

A word of caution: it is vital to manage your own expectations about what can be achieved with specific advice from different sources. Empathy and sympathy do not always equate with useful, practical help that will be of value. Likewise the most useful practical advice may not come from the most sympathetic source. Be realistic about what individuals and organisations can do for you and how you can utilise their advice: your journey to recovery is not going to be without frustrations. It is really up to you to seek the right advice from the right person at the right time, which will depend on your individual circumstances. Therefore what follows is not meant as a linear timeline or a prescribed order in which to contact people, but as a guide to all the possible, worthwhile options.

The main groups of people who can help you if your work is making you ill are:

- Your GP

- Occupational health services

- Your employer

- Employee Assistance Programmes

- Psychological support (for mental *and* physical health needs)

- Unions

- Legal advice services

Your GP

A vast number people go to their GP for help when they are ill as a result of their job, which is why I felt compelled to put pen to paper and write this book. Whether you are fatigued and burnt out from crazy hours in a role you love or you are not able to sleep because of a bullying colleague, having an objective and confidential medical opinion can be exceedingly valuable.

Although I would have expected and recommend that people talk to family or friends first, as the easiest place to start, sometimes it may be easier to approach your doctor even before you are able to bring up your illness with your loved ones or friends. This may be so particularly if you are concerned about the stigma of a mental health condition or being taken seriously with work-related stress. It is very much a personal preference, and will depend where and with whom you will feel the most at ease.

There are a number of psychological and practical reasons why confiding in your GP can be a good place to start these difficult discussions. Your GP can:

1. provide a place to acknowledge, gain affirmation and open up the conversation

2. diagnose the condition you have

3. investigate and treat physical health issues

4. treat mental health conditions

5. organise logistics, for example sick notes.

Seeking advice and help from your doctor because you believe you are ill as a result of your job is no different from attending for any other health complaint, and should afford the same pathway of diagnosis, treatment and support.

The opportunity to speak freely and confidentially in a doctor's room can offer a huge relief in itself. Even when an issue feels stigmatised or shameful elsewhere, it should not within the confines and safe space of a consultation. Even though it can be a hard admission to make to friends and family, and perhaps to yourself, admitting that your work is making you ill should feel more comfortable with a doctor. Given that almost half a million people suffer with work-related stress, anxiety or depression, there is a very high chance your doctor has seen patients very similar to you before – and some will see one or two patients in this predicament each week. A doctor will offer no judgement and can remove all shame from the situation, as you are treated in the same way as anyone suffering an illness, with compassion and sympathy. It would be treated no differently from all the other so-called 'embarrassing' conditions that a doctor sees, which are in fact not embarrassing or shameful at all.

Even if you are given no more than 10 minutes to talk with a GP, as is often the case, those few minutes can be therapeutic and worthwhile. Admitting you have an issue with your work, both to yourself and to someone else you can trust, is the start of a process of acceptance, treatment and moving on.

A diagnosis in the context of work-related ill health can be essential. The objective opinion can be valuable in many ways but especially as you don't want to miss another equally important or significant diagnosis. The typical bowel symptoms or headaches people get through work-related stress, for example, could actually underlie an entirely separate serious medical condition or another simultaneous problem. As with any illness it is important to get that diagnosis correct and not to miss anything. It could be easy to mistake weekday abdominal pain as being precipitated by the difficult relationship you have with your boss; however, a GP needs to establish that the pain isn't actually coming from the gluten you eat every day in the work canteen.

Accurate diagnosis is particularly important if you are suffering mental health symptoms. It can be difficult as the sufferer to differentiate between what you may simply brush off as 'stress' and what is actually full-blown anxiety or depression; it can be hard to see this in yourself. GPs go through specific diagnostic tools to definitively diagnose these: this is vital for the appropriate treatment.

Another reason to get a formal diagnosis of work-related ill health is that when work is making you ill, further down the line things can get complicated with employers, sick leave and even your rights as an employee. It could even come to grievance proceedings or an employment tribunal. Sadly I have seen this on occasion, and I have also seen that it is vital to have documented proof of your illness and what has been going on. The chances are you won't need this evidence but it can be useful and is a good insurance policy going forward.

Likewise, if you are going to need a fit note or a sick note in the future, your medical records need to reflect your illness and what has been diagnosed in order for your doctor to legitimately issue one. A GP cannot write a sick note or a fit note without a good background history and notes of your condition. Essentially having documented proof of your condition is sensible in terms of logistics as well as diagnosis and treatment.

There is a grave concern among people, which is totally understandable, that getting help for a mental health condition from a doctor involves being issued tranquillising medication or becoming addicted to sleeping tablets. In fact, gone are the days when people were started on sleeping tablets for insomnia during a stressful time, only to return two decades later still addicted to them. Doctors are far more pragmatic and cautious now in their approach to issuing medication and treating mental health conditions. If you have some symptoms of stress, but without a vast impact on your quality of life or functioning, a doctor would be unlikely to initiate medication. We start antidepressant medication very very cautiously, and often quite reluctantly, only when it is really essential and we have diagnostic proof to back up the need. Very strict guidelines are used to determine who needs such medication; it is not simply used as a sticking plaster to solve a problem.

Usually medication is not a solution to a problem; it is a temporary essential tool to help you feel able to cope with a situation, adopt self-help changes and perhaps see a path clearly. This is particularly the case, for example, if you can't take time off work yet are having to cope with insomnia. That scenario is a recipe for a worsening downward spiral: no sleep leads to anxiety, and anxiety leads to even less sleep. This makes it very difficult to think clearly and be motivated to change or fix your situation. The short-term help with medication in this case will not fix the problem, but it can break the cycle to allow some clarity and respite, enough to forge a better path towards recovery. Doctors do not issue medication in this situation lightly: going on to any medication is a big commitment and of course confers disadvantages as well as benefits. But it can be essential to your health.

Whatever physical health conditions you are suffering with, your GP should be the starting point to initiate treatment. Whatever is going to happen with your job and working-life, this is a given. GPs also now have access to a range of psychological interventions and mental health treatment for their patients, and you often need to see a doctor first to access these. However, there are also now many places you can access psychological support from without going through your doctor, and this is dealt with later (see page 119).

Occupational Health Services

The likelihood is that before you suffered from work-related ill health, you will never have encountered any occupational health services.

Occupational health is a specific specialism of doctors and healthcare professionals who consider and treat the range of effects that an individual's work has on their health. It is also their job to explore whether your health, fitness and well-being will affect your performance or capability within a particular job. Their role is to make sure that work is in no way damaging or compromising your health, and foster ways to ensure it doesn't.

Occupational health professionals have a role in preventing work-related ill health primarily, and are focused on your health specifically in the context of you as an employee: if you think work is a factor in your health, then occupational health should definitely be involved. They will need to know about other aspects of your health and outside work circumstances too, just like any doctor you would see.

Depending on your employer, occupational health provision can vary from nothing at all to a full-time team. Usually occupational health is provided at your place of work, but it can now be outsourced to outside agencies to offer the service. The occupational health team at work may consist of a nurse and a GP or specialist occupational health physician but it can also include physiotherapists or psychologists in some places. It very much depends on the size of your company.

The beauty of speaking to an occupational health team within your place of work is the unparalleled understanding they will have of your work situation and the structures and environment that could be affecting your health. That is not as easy for an outsider, such as your GP or your family, to appreciate. Because of their unique position within your workplace, they are well placed to deal with work-related ill health as well as the issues that can be the root cause. They will also know about the health and safety policies within your workplace, and the relevant legal regulations, and can work with you and your employer to structure your recovery and the adaptations you need.

The big question and concern people have in seeking

advice from the occupational health team is: what information goes back to the employer? The occupational healthcare professionals you see are bound by the same confidentiality agreements that exist between all healthcare professionals and their patients. The professional body for occupational health specialists requires members to 'keep all individual medical information confidential, releasing such information only with the individual's informed consent, or when required by law or overriding public interest'. So even if a company doctor was going to advise changes to your working pattern to your boss for the sake of your health, he cannot reveal your medical condition as well, unless he has your consent to do so. Even the most simple opinion of being 'fit to work' or 'needing time off' is bound by this and needs your agreement to be shared.

Occupational health physicians, however, are not personal doctors like GPs, and have to give advice to both you and your employer that is fair. For this reason, you may be asked for your consent to share information at the beginning of your consultation – you need to be very clear about what consent you are giving and what you are allowing to be shared. There are certainly instances where the occupational health consultations within companies can only go ahead once you have given consent to share information with employers. It should be possible only to share the most basic detail that will be helpful to you, but you need to explore this and be very sure of it at the outset.

The ideal outcome from seeking occupational health advice is a plan of how to tackle your work-related ill health holistically. The doctors are in a position to offer the medical aspects of the solution, such as referring you for therapy, as well as the workplace changes that need to be accepted. I have seen many instances where occupational health has really provided the foundation and support for the recovery process, allowing someone to continue working but to get better at the same time. It is a great skill to weigh up employment priorities and individual health needs successfully, but it can be achieved with a good occupational health team, a willing employee and a cooperative employer.

You can access occupational health support specifically to allow a report to be compiled regarding your work-related ill health and what needs to be done going forward in terms of your working life. This can be an incredibly valuable process, setting out the structure for both treatment and work adaptations that can aid your recovery. This plan would be produced for your manager and you would have to give full consent for this, and consent as to what you will allow to be disclosed. It is your right to see exactly what is in the report before it is shared.

If you are considering taking sick leave, then occupational health along with HR may also undertake what is known as sickness-absence management: rather than just being left to your own devices while on sick leave, and the company left to struggle, absence management involves a proper process and policy of managing the sick leave. This would include who you have to report to, monitoring your health and treatment, and appropriate planning to fill the gaps at work. You may be obliged to engage with the occupational health team in this situation.

Smaller companies and employers understandably may not have the capacity or resources to offer occupational health services. If this is the case your employer or GP should be able to offer you advice through the government scheme called Fit for Work. This offers occupational health advice and support to those who do not have the facility at work or who work for themselves. However, it is only available in instances where you have been on sick leave, or potentially could be, for a month or more.

Your Employer

Approaching your employer directly about your work-related ill health will seem like a huge and daunting step to take. Ideally it should not be the first conversation you have about your current situation and really should follow initial discussions you have already had with loved ones or healthcare professionals. Fundamentally it is not a dialogue you want to enter without a practice run in a more comfortable and 'safer' environment. It needs to be done right and with due process from the outset.

Talking to your employer about a work-based problem is not going to be easy and can seem overwhelming and frightening; it is complicated by fears of jeopardising yourself and your income, making your situation even worse than it is and losing your job. Depending on the environment and work culture within your job, disclosing this very personal information can feel like admitting a weakness, affecting your position at work and your self-esteem. Everyone in this position worries about how it will affect their performance management and whether it could lead to disciplinary proceedings.

Reassuringly however, in the majority of cases I have seen, it has been an essential hurdle to overcome in order to foster the ongoing recovery and has had no negative consequences. There may seem to be a number of reasons *not* to speak to your employer, in terms of compromising yourself, but there are also many reasons why it is good to have that conversation:

- The conversation allows you to get the support you need, or the adaptations you may require, and therefore is essential for you to remain in work.

- You may be revealing a problem your employer was unaware of but can easily and quickly address with minimal inconvenience to you or them.

- It may well be something they have dealt with before and so have all the facilities to help you already in place.

- Your employer will respect your openness and honesty, and that can encourage them to accommodate your needs in the future.

- Most employers are reasonable, understanding and want to look after their staff because it is the right thing to do (regardless of the fact that they are obligated to). If you want to be cynical, they also need you to be well as it is better for them in terms of productivity.

- It is usually far easier for an employer to offer adaptations and support early on in an illness, rather than deal with sick leave further down the line, which is costly and inconvenient.

- Your employer can offer you a referral to occupational health or time off to see a GP and get the medical help you need.

You have to establish at the outset the correct process for having this conversation – whether it is directly with your line manager, which it usually would be, or whether you go to human resources. Of course, if you are working within a toxic environment and your manager is the source of the problem, this is going to determine who and where these conversations start. It may be that bypassing a specific individual is necessary, whatever formal systems are in place. A respect for the due process is important though, whatever the circumstances.

Talking about work-related ill health is not to be done as an impromptu discussion on the shop floor, compromising both you and your colleagues. It deserves ring-fenced time and it is very important to follow any procedure within your work to protect yourself and respect the systems that exist. There is a high chance that this will not be the first time your employer has dealt with your scenario, and managers are obliged to follow procedure for such matters.

You need to enter into a conversation with your employer prepared and ready to give an explanation. While you don't want to bombard them with a file of evidence – that would appear confrontational – it can be valuable to have a short summary to hand. This can be useful both as an aide-memoire and to give some definitive points to put forward: if you have been formally diagnosed with something it is important to be clear and concise about that diagnosis and accurate in how you refer to it. Ideally you want to be honest and clear, but brief.

You want to be able to have a conversation with your employer that is non-emotive and blame-free, factual and not confrontational. There does not need to be any assumption that this will be a hostile or awkward conversation. I have come across many cases over the last few years where employers have fought admirably to get their employees back to health, and on many occasions it has been the boss who has provided the solutions that have worked and generated a recovery. Definitely do not assume that just because it is work that is making you ill, that your employer will not want or be able to help you: often they are very much the answer.

Discussions with your employer in terms of what they can do to help need to be very specific, and it can be helpful to understand what they can and can't offer in terms of your health and employment. Reasonable adjustments can be considered within your job in order to keep you in work and protect your health, but of course they can only be offered if they are viable within your workplace. Possibilities of work adaptations include changing duties and demands; reducing workloads; changing or reducing hours or allowing you to work from home; moving roles within the same department or moving department within the same company. These are merely suggestions and are not guaranteed to be possible or valuable; your expectations have to be realistic in terms of what they 'should' be able to offer you, and what they actually 'can' do in reality.

It may be helpful for you to know that your employer is required to look at the health risks you are exposed to at work. The 1999 Regulations for the Management of Health and Safety at Work state that all employers must assess the health and safety risks to which employees are exposed. These would include being exposed to stress at work and conditions that have precipitated physical or mental health problems. A stress risk assessment can be undertaken by your employer to evaluate the areas you are concerned could be the issue, allowing them to offer measures and a plan that could help. Ideally this would be something you could work through with your manager and follow to help your recovery.

In an ideal scenario, you should be able to have a frank discussion with your employer and be able to establish how they can offer help and support, formulating a plan between the two of you that minimises inconvenience for them while improving your situation and health.

Employee Assistance Programmes

An Employee Assistance Programme, or EAP, is a set of services within your workplace designed to support staff, with the aim of improving wellness and therefore functioning and performance at work. Their aim is dual-focused: they exist to improve productivity for an employer, but equally to identify and help resolve personal issues for employees that could be affecting performance. They are focused on the health and well-being of the employee but the reasoning behind their existence is really because that is good for business! That is no bad thing: if your employer has invested in their employees' health and well-being in this way, it illustrates that they are aware of the importance of healthy, happy staff. It is a positive indication of a good employer and sets the scene for accepting and acknowledging the vital interplay between work and health.

It is very likely within many companies, workplaces and public-sector organisations that an EAP will be available to you and could help in some way with a work-related illness. It would certainly be worth exploring what services are available via the EAP as it will often include help with concerns relating to health, addiction, stress, personal issues and even relationship problems. They can offer direct assistance to you for personal issues via counselling, referring on to a specialist, support and information.

EAP services may be offered within your workplace via the human resources or occupational health departments, or they may be offered externally, by an outside service provider your employer has paid for. This would be a facility you can access directly and confidentially, either online or by phone, where you can be given mental health input from psychologists and other professionals as well as counselling and other support; for example, for addiction.

An EAP can offer you help and signposting to a range of solutions that can be a small or significant part of your recovery process, such as:

- Counselling or psychological services, often specifically for stress

- Support and advice on emotional and work–life issues

- Legal advice

- Information on childcare and carers

- Financial advice

- Drug and alcohol support

- Onward referral for diagnosis and treatment

The services on offer through an EAP are definitely something to explore if you believe your job is making you ill. Often considered a 'perk' of a job, the services they provide can be hugely valuable and can include therapy and help that may not be available or so easy to access anywhere else.

Essentially, if your job is making you ill, you should see the EAP as a gateway to a range of help and services that could benefit you. An EAP can offer fast and easy access to sources of help, which is not often the case when accessing mental health services elsewhere, either via the NHS or privately. When you are feeling unwell through work and looking to forge a solution, fast access can be just what you need and want. For anyone having difficulty seeing a GP for any reason, whether for convenience or personal preference, using an EAP may allow you to bypass the step of needing a GP appointment to initiate treatment.

Psychological Support

You can access psychological support for yourself directly, without going through a middle man such as a GP or EAP.

Psychological support comes in many forms and offers many different things, from listening and 'me too' in a patient support group to fully blown psychological therapy. It can be as simple as a coffee with a friend or as formal as an appointment with a psychiatrist. Thankfully, due to the growing acceptance and understanding of mental health in the twenty-first century, there are a lot of resources available and a range of support that could be of value and suited to you and your personality. Groups are not for everyone, but equally some people want the comfort of seeing another human being.

While there is yet to be a website 'WorkStressRUs', there are a range of services and support networks you can access online. Online access offers so many advantages to people in terms of convenience, privacy and timely access to the exact help you need when you want it. The online community is there when nobody else might be, when you are stressed and anxious at midnight for example. That can be exceedingly beneficial.

Peer support is very valuable when you are feeling unwell as a result of your work. The power of 'me too' and 'this happened to me' is very significant, both emotionally and practically. There are forums online to engage with people and offload privately and confidentially in a way you may not have been able to with friends or family. Online communities, such as Elefriends and Big White Wall, in particular, allow you to talk about your stress and your mental health in a safe space (see Resources, page 216, for details).

Group support in person (not online), is a very individual preference and something people either feel comfortable with or they don't. The idea of sitting in a circle and admitting your diagnosis or problems will horrify some, but for others it provides a therapeutic and comforting haven of support. It has a massive role to play within the arena of mental health treatment for many conditions (and actually for physical health conditions as well) but is not to everyone's taste. You can find local support groups for stress and mental health conditions online or via the mental health charity Mind, who have a good knowledge of local services. Group support in the form of a 12-step programme, for example, should be an essential step if you are coping specifically with an addiction, however, as it is well known and proven to work.

You can engage with the whole range of one-to-one psychological therapies directly without the need to go through a third party. If you are looking for a face-to-face therapist you must know exactly what you need in the first instance – the specific therapies suitable for your condition are explored in Chapter 2 so you can identify the correct one. If you are doing this alone you need to ensure you use someone registered who has a good track record, and who charges a reasonable price. While a recommendation from a friend is always useful, it only works in this situation if your friend has had the same condition as you: a counsellor who has been wonderfully helpful during a bereavement may not be the appropriate professional if you have diagnosed anxiety, for example. This can prove a costly, inconvenient and frustrating mistake, and it is one I have seen happen.

It may be worth exploring what you need using websites such as www.welldoing.org or www.itsgoodtotalk.org.uk, where you can identify the right therapist for you. Make sure you look for registered professionals that are accredited with the appropriate professional body, such as the British Association for Counselling and Psychotherapy, the British Association for Behavioural and Cognitive Psychotherapies, or the Royal College of Psychiatrists. You need to have a clear idea of the price and the length of treatment you may be offered, at the outset.

Another option for directly accessing therapy can be from your computer. There are numerous programs and sites now that offer computerised cognitive behavioural therapy (CBT) for treatment of anxiety and depression. This route has some obvious advantages in terms of convenience and time, as well as cost, although it is still considered to be less effective than engaging with a professional therapist. They are usually self-help CBT courses and will really suit you if you are motivated and keen to get going on recovery – they are proven to be clinically effective and are available to anyone. The well-established program Beating the Blues is in fact recommended by the National Institute for Health and Care Excellence (NICE) for the treatment of mild to moderate depression (see Resources, page 216, for more details).

If you are physically ill as a result of your work, do not underestimate the need for emotional support. As a result of my experience in general practice, I am a huge believer in the use of charities, patient support associations and peer help for anyone suffering with any physical or mental health condition. Often the most useful thing that comes out of a consultation with a patient with eczema, for example, is the referral to the Eczema Society, where there is support, advice and guidance far beyond the scope of what a GP or other professional can offer.

If you are suffering with a physical health condition, it is worth finding the national charity or support group association, even if you simply spend an hour perusing their advice online. The specific guidance, insider knowledge and recommendations are incredibly useful, offering practical and realistic wisdom from the patient's point of view. Specifically for work-related issues, there are often areas of these sites with advice about coping with work, suggestions you can make to employers regarding your illness, and advice on how to cope within day-to-day work life. Fellow sufferers have a wealth of knowledge to share: even within a health-care setting we now use 'expert patients' to advise and guide other patients, as their dedication and knowledge can be so beneficial. The dedicated health condition charities can offer telephone support, patient forums, local support groups or simply online advice and leaflets.

Unions

The function of any union is to guard and improve conditions for their members, and that very much includes how working conditions can affect an employee's health. One of their fundamental aims is to protect members and ensure workplaces are safe: this includes acknowledging that work can put people's health at risk not just in terms of their physical health from accidents and injuries, but also stress-related conditions. Unions across the board recognise stress in the workplace as a significant issue and work locally and nationally to reduce the problem.

Speaking to your union representative can help to clarify your rights within work, and they can offer advice and solutions going forward specifically directed at improving your working conditions. Your union will be au fait with the relevant legislation and local policy within your workplace, and can therefore help in discussions about what it is reasonable to expect your employer to change, but also what exactly your employer is responsible for.

If your job is making you ill, then your union should really know about it – this is key in terms of getting you the help you need personally, but also in broader terms. Unions work at workplace, local and national levels to ensure the rights of their members, and that includes their members' rights to a work environment that does not cause them harm, including illness. Awareness of an individual's issues can highlight to them a more systemic or larger-scale problem that needs addressing.

Depending on your union and your workplace, a union can offer support in a number of different ways. It is worth exploring with their main helpline or website what is on offer specifically for you, before seeking what you are entitled to at work. Locally you should aim to make contact with your union representative or the safety representative.

The help that may be available to you from your union includes:

- Support, advice and guidance for you personally regarding work-related issues.

- Investigation into the problem that is making you ill. This may include establishing if there are any others affected.

- Helping you to formulate what to do next within the correct procedures.

- Advising you on your legal and employment rights with work-related ill health.

- Signposting you to legal specialists – often union membership will come with some degree of legal help included.

- Signposting to health and safety specialists – some will offer helplines specifically relating to health and bullying. This may be a separate service or a part of an EAP.

- Support when speaking to management – a union representative can accompany you and represent you in any meetings.

Anyone speaking to management about an issue has the right to be accompanied by another person, and a union representative is well placed to do that. Seeking union help formalises an issue and can be exceedingly valuable – their focus is on you as an employee and ensuring you are safe at work. The local union representative or safety representative will know of other issues and will ensure your problem is dealt with both for your own sake, but also for the health of the whole team going forwards.

Legal Advice Services

Seeking legal advice should not form a part of your recovery process if your job is making you ill but, as I have witnessed on more than one occasion, it is sometimes sadly necessary. Therefore a chapter entitled 'Who can help you?' would not be complete without reference to it. Most people will not need legal help. Taking legal action can be very expensive, time-consuming and stressful, so it is not something one should enter into lightly.

Resorting to the law thankfully is not common for most people who are ill as a result of their work, but if it is necessary, in among the distress of being unwell and all the other emotions job-related ill health brings, you can find yourself confused and baffled about where to turn for legal help.

In the first instance, you may be able to seek advice through your union or other professional body. Unions often offer legal assistance to members, providing advice and support on aspects including bullying and harassment, dismissal, contracts and grievances. They should be able to offer the appropriate support if you need to face an employment tribunal.

If you are not covered by a union, the best place to start for legal advice is with Citizens Advice, who can help you

with your rights relating to your workplace, dismissals, grievances, tribunals and conciliation. They offer huge amounts
of advice online, and locally face to face they can direct you
to legal advice whether from a law centre or a solicitor, or
suggest alternatives such as ACAS, the Advisory, Conciliation
and Arbitration Service. They can advise right at the outset
about what you may be entitled to and, importantly, how
much the process should and could cost you.

Knowing who to talk to and accessing their help can be an
essential part of recovering your health. Seeking the right
advice from the right person at this difficult time in your
working life may make all the difference to your healing. It
may seem intimidating to approach your employer or speak
to a therapist for the first time, but it can be incredibly valuable and worthwhile.

The next step is finding the right way to help yourself.

•

CHAPTER 6

How to Help Yourself

When work is a source of illness, most people are not in the position where they can simply get up and walk out in order to heal themselves and recover. You therefore have to foster a recovery that is built around and alongside your job, concentrating on what you can do for yourself without jeopardising your work, your career or your income. This may sound like a daunting prospect but it is achievable and I have seen it work with many of my patients.

So far we have looked at the outside help you can seek if your job is making you ill. This is now the moment to concentrate on self-help: what you can do for yourself to improve your mental and physical health by nurturing and healing your body and your mind. Part of your treatment may be to seek medical or professional help; part may involve conversations with your employer or occupational health specialist. But the self-help programme that you alone can initiate will form the essential foundation of your treatment and is the mainstay of your recovery. It will also help to promote and protect your health in the future.

This plan will not alter or correct the issues you have at your work, the problems or the negative situations: it is about changing yourself and your lifestyle to cope better with those situations and, crucially, how your mind and body reacts to them. The idea is to build up your mental and physical strength, constructing a layer of protection around you so you are stronger to deal with what life and work throws at you. There are many different areas of your life that you can explore to do this. Conversations you can have with employers and occupational health teams may rectify work issues; self-help cannot do that. This is about undertaking changes and adopting behaviours to build up your reserve of strength mentally and physically. This will improve your health and allow you to deal with stress.

The lifestyle changes and goals you now need to undertake foster strength and health but in different ways. Some are scientifically proven to be part of the treatment of particular conditions – for example, exercise as an adjunct to the treatment of mental health conditions. This self-help strategy literally makes you better. Other aspects are aimed at building up your emotional strength or resilience, allowing you to cope better so that the stress you are under has less of an impact on your health. This also makes you feel better, but indirectly: more accurately, it allows you to feel less ill.

Building up your resilience, both physically and emotionally, will play a large part in your recovery. Resilience is the ability to cope, survive and thrive when difficulties arise. Some of that is inherent, but resilience can also be built and developed. We know that resilience comes from positive relationships and a support network; certain lifestyle aspects such as relaxation; positive thinking; and taking control. Many of the following self-help strategies promote these essential building blocks of resilience in big and small ways.

Taking control is now so important. After a chapter concerned with who else can help and support you, this whole chapter focuses on what *you* can do for *yourself* and it is no coincidence that it forms a substantial part of the book. Being ill and being under pressure makes you feel out of control, but by adopting some lifestyle measures for yourself, you can take back some control of your working life and your health. Being in control even within a seemingly trivial aspect of your non-working life will help you grow strength and confidence, and can help you to feel you can claw control back elsewhere as well.

In addition, because one aspect of your life has effectively 'gone wrong' you should look to build successes and goals elsewhere. This helps to keep work-related problems in perspective and allows you to maintain your confidence and self-worth. Illness can be all-consuming, especially when it is tied in with another large chunk of your life that is your job; having goals, aims and triumphs outside that allows it to be less all-consuming, keeping your mood and energy levels up.

This chapter includes what will seem like huge ideas, and what will seem like tiny ones. Both have equal place in the realm of recovery and self-help. It is often impossible to change the big stuff (and that is very true with many people I have seen facing difficult working circumstances), but looking at changing some very slight, small things can be hugely valuable. These micro-actions are easy for you to adopt and, crucially, easy to sustain and succeed at. For example, making yourself a wholesome packed lunch may seem trivial given the illness and the job difficulties you are facing, but ideas like this are not. These small, minor changes and micro-successes will add up together and can start to improve what otherwise feels like an impossible situation.

Each micro-success brings with it a tiny piece of positive momentum and some confidence, which become the springboard to the next positive micro-change, which again brings about positive momentum and increased self-worth and confidence. The positivity continues to grow and allows you to build more and more. This generates a positive cycle that is really important when you come from the weak point of illness and gives you a feeling of 'I can do this'. That power and confidence from the micro-actions can help you take the leap to make bigger changes, have the bigger conversations and change the more significant aspects you may need to deal with. Or they will simply make you feel good, feeding into your resilience and constructing your recovery.

There are a lot of ideas presented in this chapter and that may feel overwhelming. Coming from the low point of ill health, trying to take on board all the ideas that now follow will be impossible. Some concepts may not fit into your life; some things may not be for you or will not be something you want to contemplate. To start, just try one area to explore or change and see how you get on. Then add something else and build up, changing those aspects that you can, you enjoy and that fit in with your life. Set yourself up for success, not failure: you don't want to try to make too many unrealistic changes which then don't succeed. Take things slowly and simply to build up your recovery and resilience at your own pace.

When your job is making you ill, there are many areas you can choose to focus on to make yourself better – I would recommend you consider them all as possible pathways to better health. Changing or improving these areas of life have been proven to improve health; this could be a reduction in physical health symptoms, or an improvement in mood or self-esteem. And I have seen these work time and time again with my own patients in clinic. You can make a tangible difference and bring about your own recovery. These are the well-established areas in which you could consider changes:

- Your relationships

- Diet

- Exercise

- Sleep

- Your journey to work

- Relaxation

- Your phone and internet use

- Planning your schedule

Nurture Your Relationships

If your job is making you ill, then building up and focusing on your relationships is absolutely vital. I cannot emphasise enough just how fundamental, strong and supportive interpersonal relationships are to your well-being and recovery. If you are trying to build up and repair your health, then you need to make sure your network of relationships is subject to the same tender loving care.

We know from countless studies that support, family and relationships are good for your physical health and can be protective against certain physical illnesses. Social isolation and loneliness are bad for your health: research shows that having more or better quality relationships is related to a reduced risk of mortality in the elderly. That is pretty strong stuff. Some research analyses point to a lack of social relationships as being as big a risk factor for poor health as smoking, obesity and a lack of exercise. Fundamentally, humans are social creatures, and we require that social need to be fulfilled in order for us to be healthy as well as happy.

Healthy interpersonal relationships are a vital part of resilience – your ability to thrive, survive and cope with difficulties. This will not be news to anyone who has shared a problem, cried on a friend's shoulder or felt the empathy of a supportive partner. Going through anything alone, or feeling alone, is tough. We know that healthy relationships enable your resilience at work, whether that is through the support or mentorship of a good manager or friendship with work colleagues. Any supportive relationship you invest in will improve your confidence and self-worth, and consequently your mental health.

Relationships of any kind can get into a rut or a mess which can be hard to see when you are faced with the all-consuming cloud that is ill health and a job that is making you ill, so you have to make time to nurture them. Relationships, particularly the home ones, can be detrimentally affected by work stress, illness and the fallout that brings; people change and withdraw through illness, feel less motivated, less interested in fun, more irritable and angry. Of course this will all have a big impact on marriage particularly, as well as our other significant relationships. Negativity tends to have a snowball effect: work and health go awry, then your relationship goes wrong as well as a result. This can be hard to see when you are in the middle of it, especially when there are bigger issues such as a difficult job to concentrate on. But you need to make your relationships a priority for TLC, and focus on them as a part of the holistic process of making yourself better.

Relationships, family ties, friendships and our personalities are so varied and wide-ranging that it is hard to prescribe or direct exactly how spending more time or investing in a relationship can be fostered. The simple generic message would be to invest some time to connect more. In practice this means:

1. **Spending quality time with your family and loved ones** When scheduling your week, even a crazy working week, make room for the people in your life that you want to see, who make you feel good, and spend quality time with them. Nothing complicated, nothing expensive and nothing necessarily planned: just good, old-fashioned, non-distracted, uninterrupted time, whatever that may be. Quality time is an expression that is overused now but that is what you want: special time connecting with those around you who support and nurture you. Stop what you are doing and make space for them and your relationship. Prioritise it, and make sure you are doing that every day. Far too often we sail through busy weeks and think we're spending time with our family when we're actually just living together. Purposefully take the time to connect.

2. **Getting in touch with your friends** How often have you said to a friend 'speak soon' and you really mean it, but actually you don't get round to it for a long time? With hectic schedules and weeks, our precious time with good friends can be washed away through no fault of our own. When you're ill, particularly with depression, it is hard to motivate yourself to see friends and do things you previously enjoyed. Start with a regular phone call and build up. You are starting to rebalance your time by adding in what is protective and healthy, and prioritising connecting with a friend or loved one is just that.

3. **Socialising** Making the effort to see people socially should be a priority for your mental health: in your mind set yourself the target of making an arrangement at least once a week to spend time with a friend and take on the responsibility to do this. Have a 'friendship

audit'. Are there people you relish spending time with, who you don't see enough for whatever reasons? Get in touch with them and make a date with them. It might seem unnecessary and childlike to plan friendships but it isn't: being proactive about your relationships will make you feel good and is worth investing your time in for the improvement of your mental health.

4. **Spending time with your colleagues** Connecting with people at work is hugely important for resilience, particularly when work has become a source of illness for you. Some more enlightened companies champion this and set up workplace environments to encourage it. As much as you can, try to do this for yourself. Take the chance to have a break with someone and sit and talk with them, or find out about mentoring and support schemes. Simply just focus on good relationships at work and what you can do to encourage them across the spectrum of people you work with. Even if work is generally a source of tension for you, you can foster relationships within work that offer some respite from that and some amelioration of the stress.

When you are well, friendships and good relationships happen naturally, usually with no premeditation or forethought. But when you are ill they need to be nurtured and empowered as a fundamental part of your recovery.

Diet

When you are stressed, not feeling well, or are emotionally and physically drained it will seem hard to focus on something as simple and banal as what you are eating.

Food is a comfort and many of us eat emotionally. At the end of a long or terrible day evening treats can seem like all there is to look forward to. When stress is taking over, comfort often appears in the form of alcohol, a takeaway pizza or a large bag of crisps. During a hard working day it can be bliss-ful to take a 5-minute break and relish sugary snacks or a large coffee. And conversely the opposite can often be true: I have met many patients unwell through work or other life issues who don't eat. People who may avoid food all day to binge in the evening, or those who can't stomach eating well during a hectic day and then don't have the energy to make anything decent to eat in the evening. Often with stress, anxiety or physical ill-health issues like IBS, people cannot actually face food from a fear of symptoms such as tummy pain or diar-rhoea. With people who are anxious or suffering from stress, the overwhelming feeling of nausea can curb any appetite and making eating anything, never mind good food, a chore. Depression often comes with a reduced appetite as a common symptom and it can be very difficult to motivate yourself back into eating even with family and partner support.

The relationship between our happiness, our mood and our diet is very strong. Therefore focusing on your diet has to be a part of any recovery. Taking some time to adopt some healthy habits, even one or two positive dietary changes, can reap significant rewards. By concentrating on your diet you are improving your health physically of course, but you are also nurturing yourself mentally.

This is not about a complete diet overhaul, which would be overwhelming for anyone and especially someone who is unwell. You are looking to make some modifications that are achievable and sustainable and are specifically aimed at helping to improve your health – especially your mental health – rather than weight loss. Here are some easy ways to start.

1. **Maintain your blood sugar level** The strong relationship between how and what we eat and how we feel is largely down to the physiology of how our blood sugar levels are maintained. Our food is converted into blood sugar for our body's cells to use: if blood sugar levels drop people noticeably feel fatigued, irritable and can even feel low. We would all recognise those symptoms from episodes of not eating. But changes in blood sugar can also cause those mood changes, especially if sugar levels are swinging between high and low throughout the day. High-sugar products, quick-release sugary treats and drinks make your blood sugar peak and trough pretty quickly, leading your levels to be in a continual state of fluctuation: if you are already feeling wobbly or low, that will only contribute to your mood disturbance. If you are already under strain from life stressors on your mood, you don't want to add to that further with mood changes from food. Instead you want to keep things as stable as you can. You can achieve this by opting for foods that maintain your blood sugar at a more constant level and avoiding those that make it spike. Slow release energy foods such as brown complex carbohydrates, wholegrains, vegetables and proteins are better choices for meals and snacks than quick bursts of energy from sugary products.

2. **Eat mindfully** Eating is not only about physical nourishment, but mental nourishment and resilience. So whether you have 5 minutes or an hour, take the time to sit and eat mindfully. You are not reaping any of those benefits by grabbing your food and eating it at your desk or while you're rushing around. Especially at work, ensure you take the appropriate time for eating

and utilise it. Take the time to sit down and eat, enjoy your food and relish concentrating on yourself. If you can do this for every meal, that is a good amount of time to be focusing on yourself, on being mindful and nurturing yourself, and that can only make you feel good.

3. **Prepare yourself for a hard day of work with a proper breakfast** It is a mistake to miss breakfast or grab something in a packet as you commute. Sit down and have a proper breakfast, preferably with someone else, even if it means getting up earlier. You want to start the day from a strong position to manage better what lies ahead, and you can create that from having an energy-filled breakfast and giving yourself the time to eat it. 'Good breakfasts' come in many different forms, whether porridge, eggs, fruits or wholegrain cereals; what is important is taking the time to prepare and enjoy it for yourself. You want to avoid starting the day badly because you are already in a low-sugar slump. This is incredibly important if you are a shift worker: it may be that your breakfast is in fact your dinner, but eat wisely and mindfully so that you have good energy through your shift.

4. **Get organised** It can seem impossible within a working week and busy life to ensure you eat proper evening meals rather than junk or takeaways. The only way to get around this is with planning and organising when you do have the time. Taking the time to plan your evening meals for the week when you have time at the weekend will cultivate really good eating habits, a better diet and is yet another way that you are looking after yourself and giving yourself TLC. This is not about preparing gourmet food – you can simply

plan to have a jacket potato for dinner – but just that little bit of forethought will protect you from ordering the unnecessary takeaway and break your reliance on bad habits. Batch cooking is incredibly popular now among certain diet gurus, and simply involves making large quantities of food when you have the time and freezing it in portions. It is an ideal way of ensuring good food is there waiting for you in your freezer with very little effort needed when you are hungry and tired.

5. **Plan what you are going to eat at work** You want to eat food that releases energy slowly and doesn't cause peaks and troughs in your mood. Good carbohydrates, plenty of protein and vegetables, along with fibre and fruit, are the ideal way to do this. If you eat at a work canteen, this can be a rush and inconvenient, so would you be better off taking lunch with you? You can then avoid poor choices and take food you really enjoy but which will make you feel good. At first try this one day a week, perhaps, to see if it works for you. Of course it may not be logistically possible for everyone, and some people are fortunate enough to have a great work canteen, but if you find yourself always grabbing something on the hoof or forced to make poor food choices, then consider it. Taking snacks to work, such as nuts, fruit, yoghurt or wholegrain cereals, is also really worth it so you have something to grab when you feel the urge.

6. **Try to ensure your food is nourishing you as best it can** Aiming for your five-a-day is a good target to go for to ensure you are getting a great range of vitamins, minerals and fibre within your diet that nurture you from within. This is good for your digestive health as

well as providing vitamins that help mental health. Fruit and vegetables are also a far better alternative snack to the sugar highs from processed treats. Lacking iron can make you feel fatigued and sluggish, which affects your mood, and so it is worth ensuring you have enough in your diet from dark green vegetables such as spinach and broccoli as well as red meat if you eat it. 'Good fats', which are omega 3 and 6, are considered to be good for brain health and are found in oily fish, nuts and seeds and olive oil. If you feel you lack essential vitamins or components of a balanced diet, consider taking a supplement to boost your intake: it can be a good daily habit to get into if you are unable to eat enough through your diet.

7. **Cut down on caffeine.** Caffeine comes in the form of coffee, tea, cola and chocolate as well as energy drinks; we all rely on it and enjoy it. That is no bad thing per se, however caffeine increases your heart rate and your blood pressure, and it is a stimulant disturbing your sleep. If your body is already in a heightened state from stress hormones or anxiety, you are fuelling that state by adding in caffeine. This is tricky as often people feel they need it as a treat, a pick-me-up or an energy boost, but it can actually be worsening the way you feel, not improving it. Cutting that caffeine down can just take the edge off your increased heart rate and blood pressure, and therefore reduce how anxious or unwell you feel. You have to cut caffeine down slowly as it does cause withdrawal headaches, but often when people do cut down, they feel better surprisingly quickly. It is essential to cut caffeine out from the latter part of the day so your sleep is as optimal as it can be.

8. **Stay hydrated throughout the day** This will have a positive impact on your mood and concentration. We know that dehydration can make you feel sluggish and reduce concentration, and drinking water is the best way to avoid that. Much of your water intake comes from your diet, so you do not need to down two litres or more a day as is often quoted. To avoid dehydration and the mood effects from that you want to drink around a litre of water throughout the day. It is a good substitute for sugary and caffeine-based drinks and helps you feel refreshed, as well as being good for your digestive health. It is a really easy and cheap change to make in your diet, and a good one to start with.

9. **Change your diet** For some conditions there are certain diets that are proven to help. This would be the case for IBS, for example, which is treated with a FODMAP diet (see Chapter 3). If this applies to you, give the dietary changes as much credence as your medical and other treatments: these diets can be as powerful as any pharmaceuticals and should not be underestimated. It is also hugely empowering for you to take control of your diet as part of your treatment and to be in charge of this positive change. A therapeutic diet will take planning and organisation, particularly around a busy and difficult work schedule. But it is worth the investment in this essential part of your recovery.

Dietary changes can seem overwhelming for trivial gains, but many people are surprised by the huge impact even minor modifications can have on their mental and physical well-being.

Exercise

There is so much evidence now for the health benefits of exercise, if we could bottle it we'd be calling it a wonder drug.

It is probably not too much of an exaggeration to call exercise a panacea, and in terms of illness from work it can really improve your symptoms, no matter whether you are suffering with headaches or IBS or anxiety or depression. I would recommend it across the board to everyone, in some form, no matter what your circumstances or symptoms.

Exercise, along with dietary changes, is one of the lifestyle changes you can make that will have a significant impact on both your physical and mental health. You will be bringing about your own recovery by physically improving your health, as well as nurturing your resilience and emotional well-being.

When you are unwell or suffering in a job that is making you feel unwell, exercise may not seem like something you fancy doing or something that could possibly help the way you feel. It absolutely can. Do not make the mistake of thinking exercise is not for you right now because:

- you don't have time to exercise

- you are too tired to exercise

- sport is not your thing

- you can't afford it.

Exercise is for everyone and generates huge benefits at all times. You may think you don't have the time to exercise, but you can make time. You may feel too tired to exercise, but in fact exercise increases energy levels and improves fatigue in the long run. Exercise does not have to involve sport: it is as simple as walking, taking the stairs and ensuring you are moving around throughout the day. And something like walking is free.

Exercise is such an important aspect of treatment and preventative health it features in the formal medical guidelines for a huge range of conditions across physical and mental health.

The tangible benefits of exercise will be:

- A reduction in anxiety and stress levels and an improvement of mood. This comes in the short term with the release of hormones and endorphins (the happiness chemicals in the brain), and in the long term as the benefits build up.

- Exercise is proven to improve sleep and reduce sleeping problems in those suffering from them. It is a recognised way of helping with insomnia. Good sleep is essential to maintain a good mental state.

- Exercise prevents and treats a range of physical conditions such as diabetes, heart disease, pain conditions and high blood pressure. Being physically well allows you to be better mentally.

- Exercise affords fantastic opportunities to socialise and connect with your supportive relationships.

- Exercise allows you thinking time as you walk or swim, and an opportunity for mindfulness if you spend time in the outdoors enjoying your surroundings.

- Exercise is a great 'micro-action' that easily leads to success and the positivity that brings. Exercise, however basic, gives you a sense of achievement, helps your self-esteem and allows you to set and reach goals. This is tremendously good for your mental state and bringing about other positive changes.

If you do not take any exercise currently, then getting started can seem daunting, so at first do nothing new except walk more. This could include taking the stairs whenever you can, walking some of your journey to work (for 10–15 minutes) or taking time out of your day to go for a walk. Starting does not have to be any more complicated than that. As you start to feel fitter and notice the benefits, then add to it: walk more and make sure you are aiming for that most days. Keep a record of what you are doing so you can see what you have achieved and enjoy the sense of accomplishment from that.

Exercise does need to be added to your schedule and planned, as it is very easy for it not to happen. Even the most motivated need to make sure that they plan their exercise so there is time for it in the day and it is convenient. This can seem hard at the start, especially if your week feels very busy and your mind overly full. But it is absolutely worth it. It is even worth getting up earlier to make time to exercise, either as part of your journey to work or more formally. That may seem like a huge leap, but after it becomes your routine you will welcome the benefits it brings.

A dramatic and unrealistic exercise plan is not going to be sustainable so you have to choose exercise that you enjoy and that is convenient. You need to be able to fit it in without too much disruption so that you are reaping all the benefits without the hassle. Start small if you are starting something new and just aim for once a week at the start: you don't want to set yourself up for failure with a four times a week plan that is unrealistic. You want to set achievable targets and enjoy the feeling of the self-confidence they bring. Perhaps there is something you did as a child, like horse-riding or swimming, that you really enjoyed and you could restart again, recreating that childhood enjoyment.

Exercise can be anything that gets you moving and increases your heart rate. Of course there is a vast range to consider, weighing up costs, convenience and who you want to do it with. Many people successfully exercise every day without formally engaging with any gym or any sport, simply by walking to work or walking the dog and taking the stairs whenever they can – there's no sports kit involved but the benefits are the same. Conversely, engaging with a more formal exercise hobby such as an exercise class or a team sport is a great way to relax and wind down, to socialise and to enjoy the companionship. It can be a really worthwhile pastime and a way to adopt goals and successes outside work. There isn't a right or wrong way to do it: the focus has to simply be doing exercise that you can sustain and enjoy throughout your working week.

Exercise can mean a whole host of things depending on who you are. The most important thing is to take it on and empower it as a part of your schedule that is both therapeutic and protective for your health.

Sleep

A proper night's sleep is absolutely vital to good physical health and strong mental health. There isn't really one illness, symptom or condition that won't benefit from the proper rest resulting from a good night's sleep. It is so fundamental to us as humans and such a mundane, inconsequential part of our routine that it is easy to forget just how important and restorative it can be.

Ensuring you are sleeping well is absolutely vital if your job is making you ill, particularly if you are suffering from overwork, exhaustion and stress when rest can be elusive. If you are suffering from marked insomnia you need to follow the ideas set out in Chapter 3 to improve your sleep, and try to cure that in the long term. But anyone can improve their sleep quality and quantity and should try to do so as part of any recovery.

We all know the short-term effects of a poor night's sleep – feeling irritable, a bit low and jittery the next day – and you want to avoid even the slightest hint of that if you are already suffering upset and ill health. It is worth concentrating on sleep, not only for its restorative powers but to avoid any of the negatives that even slightly poorer sleep may bring.

There is no exact quantity that defines 'a good night's sleep' – essentially it involves you waking up feeling rested and refreshed consistently, most mornings. Not feeling like that can also be caused by stress and illness of course, particularly mental health conditions such as depression, but improving your sleep quality can only reap benefits and it is a worthy aim.

Be honest: are you really getting the best possible night's sleep for yourself? Just because you may be used to going to bed late and coping with it, there may still be room for improvement. Take the chance a few nights in a row to have an earlier night consistently and see how that makes you feel. It may be that you are not getting enough sleep but have simply become accustomed to your routine – I have seen this happen to several patients, who have been simply amazed by how much better they feel with an hour or two extra of sleep. Of course late nights are part of a normal busy routine, but ensure earlier, or early, nights are planned within your week. I really see in clinic how much people underestimate this before they try it, only to be hugely impressed with the results.

You want your sleep to be as restful and sustained as possible and that means creating the ideal environment for sleep. This is often termed 'sleep hygiene', as explained on page 70, and is about adopting measures that promote and secure sleep. It is used as a part of insomnia treatment but can ensure good sleep for us all. Your sleeping environment should be the right temperature (cooler is better) and as dark and as quiet as it can be to keep you asleep. You should remove from your bedroom anything that will disturb this: phones, LCD displays, TVs and, especially, work-related para-phernalia – psychologically such things are not restful. Think of your bed as only for sex and sleep; prioritise both of these over any other activities in the bedroom.

Although exercise is good to help you sleep well, it is too stimulating to do in the evening and should be done earlier in the day so it doesn't disturb your sleep. Ideally, in the last hour or two before bed you should also avoid eating and working, and instead opt for relaxing activities like reading or taking a bath. And of course you should not be having any caffeine, which is too stimulating and interrupts good quality sleep. (These may feel like baby steps to creating a perfect night's sleep, and that is exactly what they are: you are going back to basics to improve your health with the best night's sleep you can create.)

Urban legend would suggest that drinking alcohol is a good way to help you sleep and relax after a hard day. However, physiologically alcohol is not actually good for sleep. Although it produces that familiar dozy feeling in all of us, actually it reduces the quality of sleep you get. Alcohol can be a healthy and appropriate part of a relaxing evening routine, with a meal and socialising, but I would not recommend it as a sleep aid.

You want to optimise your sleep however you can: rather than falling asleep anywhere, anyhow and at any time, fix an established sleep routine in the best place for the best length of time. This may involve some sleep hygiene measures, or it may simply involve going to bed an hour earlier without changing anything else. It is worth trying. Sleep can very much fall into the category of 'I've always been like that, so don't need to change', but you could be missing out on better sleep, and consequently better mood and better health, without out even realising it.

Your Journey to Work

Your journey to work may well be a source of your stress and moans and groans, ruining your day twice a day. It is an essential part of the drudge, a hurdle to be jumped during the rat race of each day, and you can't avoid it. But with some relatively easy changes you can stop it being another source of woe and an additional stressor, and switch it to being something useful, even therapeutic. Your journey to work offers you something very precious and lacking in most people's day: time for yourself. You should use it to build up your health.

Whether your commute is 10 minutes or over an hour, you can use the time wisely and efficiently to help your mind relax at both ends of the day. Rather than having that window as a period of time when you're rushing, your brain racing through the day's events with the panic building up, there is no reason for it not to be a time for active relaxation, recuperation and time out.

It may seem unbelievable, but if you get your journey right you can be in the position to look forward to and relish your daily commute. That will go a long way to improving your mood, reducing your stress levels and helping you recover. Here are some key things to consider:

1. **Is your journey the best it can be?** For most people there may be no changes possible, logistically or financially, but consider whether you can ameliorate any stress that the journey causes relatively easily. Don't fall into the trap of 'I've always done it this way, I'll just carry on', but rather think about the other options – switching to doing part of the journey on foot or on public transport, for example. Are there better routes you can take that will avoid the traffic

and reduce your stress? Many people fall into the habit
of just trudging through the same awful journey each
day, not considering that there could be a better one
that is less stressful or easier. That may mean a longer
journey, but don't discount that as it may be worth it if
it is less stressful. Variety is good for your mood, rather
than spending the time on autopilot: can you alter
your journey some days to break up the routine and
the stress?

2. **Leave home earlier** When sleep and home time feels
   precious compared to work, that is a source of distress,
   the last thing you will feel like doing is going to work
   earlier – but that could be a better way to start your
   day. You may try to leave home as late as possible,
   avoiding work for as long as possible; but if you are
   already suffering from stress or illness, you don't want
   to be running out the door each day, almost missing
   buses or sitting in traffic jams as you get later and later,
   with your blood boiling. Before you have even faced
   the stress of work, your blood pressure is rising, your
   adrenalin is spiked and your heart is racing; you are
   starting the day already in stress mode. If you commit
   to leaving earlier and avoiding that unnecessary
   pressure, you are keeping your stress levels down, your
   blood pressure down and preserving your mood. You
   start the day feeling ahead, not already on the back
   foot, which is immensely powerful psychologically. It
   may come from leaving 10 minutes earlier or half an
   hour earlier; it may even involve getting up earlier, but
   it can really be worth it to start the day winning rather
   than losing.

3. **Use the time positively** In your mind and your plan
   for the week, switch your commute from being a

nightmare, hassle-filled part of the day to a time for you to treat yourself and indulge in something that will be relaxing. Whether you are walking, driving or on public transport, what can you do that will offer relaxation and stress reduction on a regular basis? Can you escape into a novel, an audio book, podcasts or your favourite music? Do what you don't normally make time for and ring-fence that journey time as a set period for this relaxation. Rather than the journey being a source of stress, it can be the time for relaxation and escapism – however that looks to you. Commit to doing this each day so it becomes a routine that nurtures you throughout the week. Many people go one step further, utilising this time for active relaxation such as practising mindfulness using an app, or meditation. Your regular journey is a wonderful period of time to do this, nurturing your mind and reducing your stress levels in this way is a mentally healthy way to start and end a working day.

4. **Try to avoid work and internet connectivity during your journey** Your journey is your personal time, not work time. Constantly being bombarded with messages and pop-ups, whether they are work emails or on your social networks, is not inherently relaxing even if it feels like it makes the journey pass quicker. You don't want to arrive at work with your thoughts and mind already racing and anxious about the day ahead; it might seem like a good use of time to plan the day ahead during your journey time but that can be done in work time. It is important to ring-fence your travel time as yours, and arrive at work feeling refreshed, not already hassled. And hassle doesn't just come from work emails: it can come from distressing headlines,

social media posts and even personal messages. Afford yourself the time to escape into relaxation on your journey rather than a constant bombardment of media.

5. **Can your journey to work also be an opportunity to exercise?** Exercise is a phenomenal adjunct to any treatment regime and is excellent for your mental and physical health. Often though, one of the reasons people give for not exercising is the time it takes, particularly with a chaotic work schedule. Any type of increased movement and exercise at either, or both, ends of the day will improve how you feel. It is a stress reliever and improves your mood, and physically it provides huge benefits. At the outset, could one journey a week involve more walking? Can you walk to the next bus stop, park further away or take the stairs? Is it safe and feasible for you to consider cycling one day a week? You may have never even considered it, but now is the time. If adding in some exercise on some days is possible, can you do so on more days, or even most days, until exercising and your journey are effectively combined? If you can start the day with walking you have already geared up the day as a success in terms of your personal goal to exercise and that feels good. At the end of the day, walking for the first part of your journey can be a great stress reliever, pounding the pavement and getting some fresh air. This is all about making your life easier and your mood better: combining travel and exercise can be a great way to do that.

Make your journey work for you as a vital part of your relaxation each day. You can make very simple changes that are hugely effective for your recovery.

Relaxation

Relaxation means mentally and physically winding down and is as important a part of rest as sleep. Relaxing is actively resting really, so you can feel yourself de-stress and be conscious of that process. Sleep is restorative of course, but properly undertaken relaxation when awake can make you feel very rested, and is therapeutic physically and mentally. Learning how to relax properly should be part of your recovery no matter what condition you are suffering from.

Relaxation means a huge range of things, from flopping in front of the TV to climbing a mountain to taking a dance class to meeting a friend. It is not something that can be prescribed: you know what you like to do to relax, you just have to make the time to do it. Prioritising a hobby or just some informal relaxation is hugely important and you should be actively making sure you do this.

Having a significant focus outside your work such as a hobby can be an incredibly valuable part of relaxation, with some significant advantages. When work is all-consuming but going well, that is great; but when work is a source of illness and pain, then if it is the main focus in your life, the negative impact will be multiplied. Having other interests to aim for and enjoy is a great way to temper this and maintain your mental well-being.

Concentrating on a pastime specifically for relaxation offers you the chance to have goals and successes outside your employment and career and ticks a lot of boxes in your recovery plan. As we have discussed, any successes feed into your feelings of self-worth and confidence, and can be taken into other areas of your life. You are building up your resilience. A hobby, no matter what that may be, offers you the chance to socialise and therefore build up your support network. It gives you a distraction from your symptoms and your troubles. It offers you variety in your week which gives you balance and perspective on other things you are facing. Challenging yourself to commit to something and achieve it simply makes you feel good. Taking on a hobby is a different way to relax and allows you to define yourself by something other than your work.

With the mood changes of mental health conditions and the symptoms of physical health problems, you can become accustomed to not relaxing or having any interests. This is because often illness comes with a feeling of what's called 'anhedonia' – losing the ability or desire to enjoy yourself, have pleasure and do fun things. It is a classic sign of depression and can lead to a spiral of isolation and worsening mood. A milder form of this can come with stress and other mental troubles – you simply lose the motivation to even arrange the fun things, or don't feel you have the energy to get up and go out to do something you really enjoy.

Actively trying to relax, timetabling it and setting it as a goal is a really important part of maintaining your mental health and building up your resilience. You are improving your emotional and physical capacity to cope with adversity by giving your mind a different outlet. Along with diet, exercise and sleep, ensuring you have specific relaxation time is an optimum way to build a recovery. This can take any form of relaxation that has always suited you, or you may need to learn a new way to relax.

Learning to relax properly is something worth taking the time for and is a very positive aspect of self-help. This is often called 'active relaxation' and involves learning approaches to positively promote mentally winding down. For example, progressive muscle relaxation can be helpful for people with anxiety and is a technique involving learning to relax each of the muscle groups in sequence, to create an overwhelming reduction in tension throughout the body. Meditation, breathing exercises and yoga would all be forms of active relaxation, as they create a feeling in the mind and body of rest, calm and peace. Some people will get that feeling automatically from a walk in the park or a relaxing bath, but if these feelings don't naturally come to you with your chosen form of relaxation, it is worth adopting active relaxation into your routine.

Mindfulness is one approach to active relaxation that everyone can try and can easily form part of a daily routine. Mindfulness may seem like a very simple and insignificant undertaking, but it is recommended in the official medical guidelines to maintaining a good mental state in those with a previous history of depression. It therefore has a scientific evidence base that it works.

Mindfulness is an awareness of the present, what you can see and feel right now to the exclusion of other thoughts. It means you are engaging your five senses and concentrating on what they are currently experiencing, rather than thinking about the past, the future or any racing thoughts. With mindfulness you notice the mundane and the usual, enjoying the sensations that you experience. If you imagine your usual walk down the road on autopilot to the bus stop, with mindfulness you would be focusing on how green the leaves are that you can see, how your muscles feel as you walk or how it feels as the wind moves your hair. You focus on very rudimentary sensations and this allows you to become aware of all the thoughts and feelings you experience at all times, which can begin to foster control over those thoughts and any destructive patterns in them. It can be hugely valuable.

Practising mindfulness can become a part of your everyday routine. It can be part of your journey to work or something you undertake when going for a walk or other exercise. It is worth taking the time for and many people will set aside time for mindfulness in the form of meditation, or use an app to help them do this and train their mind to be mindful. Creating a time in your day to be mindful can involve 10 minutes to sit silently, making yourself aware of all the sensations and feelings you are experiencing. This would be as simple as concentrating on your breathing: you can see it as a form of mental exercise which you practise every day. If it feels helpful to you in its simplest form, it may be worth taking an online or face-to-face course or exploring an app so you can further your mindfulness practice and adopt it as a part of your recovery.

Connectivity

I cannot emphasise enough how nurturing, healthy and stress-relieving it will be to disconnect your router and turn your phone off! If I could prescribe this in clinic, I would.

I truly believe that being contactable, available, switched on, disturb-able, connected, online and distract-able all the time has a negative impact on mental health and stress levels. As the body of evidence grows, experts can see that although the online world and technology confer huge advantages, they also bring with them a plethora of disadvantages. The main one in terms of mental health is constant connectivity and the impact that has on stress levels.

Within the last two decades it has become normal for us to assume we need to be contactable and switched on 24 hours a day, at weekends, on holiday and when we are supposed to be doing other things. We have all fallen into a trap of thinking we have to be available, wired up, connected and online all the time. When you are stressed, unwell or suffering, no matter what the cause, constant connectivity is an added stressor and needs to be reduced. It is another source of anxiety: your heart rate, blood pressure and stress hormone levels all go up with each update, email or text message, adding to how stressed you feel. You need to turn off, switch off and chill out: a digital detox is hugely valuable.

Connectivity unwittingly intrudes on holidays, journeys, relaxation time, mealtimes and important relationship time with children, partners and friends. It takes us away from what we should be doing and what is good for us; the overuse of digital devices has grown to the detriment of our downtime and the increase in our stress levels, as it interferes with proper relaxation and precious time to nurture relationships. It allows no space to be mindful. The relentless bombardment of messages, the perpetual vibration in your pocket or ringtone is distracting and time-consuming and takes you away from the more healthy, protective aspects of your life – relationships, family, sleep, rest and personal thinking space. With constant connectivity you are always being distracted from what you are doing and what you want to be doing: you can walk into any restaurant and see the faces of couples lit up by their phone screens to see this in action. And now we have even become accustomed to *double-screening*: being distracted from one screen with another, for example checking social media when you are watching a film.

You only have to spend time with someone with no phone or when you don't have a connection yourself, to see the value and significance of disconnecting. You become more focused, fully immersed and fully appreciative of what you are doing and who you are with. Even in my general practice, consultations are interrupted by ringtones and vibration alerts. It is a mistake to think connectivity fosters relationships; it generally interrupts and disrupts them, whatever they may be. This is a huge disadvantage when we know that relationships are so good for our health and well-being.

It is not just work emails and messages that are a distraction; it is the constant onslaught of everything – social media, personal messages, news headlines and adverts. If you are having quality time relaxing, or are with a friend, whatever the interruption, it is going to disrupt that. Having one eye on the person you are with and one eye on a phone message you quickly check, does not allow for positive relationships and keeps you in a permanently heightened state of alert, rather than the relaxing mood you want to create. You are not allowing yourself to concentrate on either properly, so the messages are not getting their proper attention and nor is the activity you're supposed to be doing. This is especially true when you are eating, as having a meal is time to relax and nurture, concentrate and be mindful of what you are doing and relish your food and the company. Even in a 10-minute lunch break, take the opportunity to wind down, not speed up.

More and more psychological evidence is building up that social media can be detrimental to mental health for our children and teenagers, and the same is true for adults. While I would be the first to advise social support networks and forums online for those suffering with physical or mental illnesses, social media is a different ball game and, I would maintain, lessens mood and certainly reduces self-confidence. No matter what your age or status in life, the onslaught of filtered and airbrushed photos and unreal status updates do nothing for anyone's self-esteem: you learn to continually compare yourself to a false reality and are constantly made to feel you are missing out. This may be the norm now but it is not healthy. We are given a warped, rose-tinted view of others' lives, creating what can only be a negative impression of our own. This is true whether you are ill or well, but when you are suffering with mood disturbance and a lack of self-worth or anxiety it is going to have a particularly bad effect. At the very minimum, it is not going to make you feel great; at worst it will worsen your mental health. What seems like a harmless forum to upload holiday snaps becomes another rat race, another pressure, more perceived failure and another source of stress and anxiety.

It is worth trying some of the following ideas to disconnect, as part of improving your mental health:

1. **Ring-fence time during the day when you will not look at your phone** It can either be switched off or on silent. A good time to start this is the time between getting up and leaving the house, or the initial period when you arrive home from work. Set a time period, maybe an hour or two and put the phone away and just get on with what you are doing, even if that is as mundane as brushing your teeth or making your dinner. Just get on and do that and allow yourself to be present in that moment and not distracted or disturbed. This only works if you also ring-fence time to be *on* the phone: plan a set period of time when you will look at the messages, indulge in those status updates and sort anything out. You are creating boundaries between time online and time offline and not merging the two. You should really aim for this every day.

2. **Do your own digital detox** You can now go on retreats which are advertised as digital detoxes with no connectivity, but you can do this yourself too. This is now so popular it has been termed a 'Digital Sabbath': taking one day to turn off all connectivity as a great way to relax and enjoy whatever you are or are not doing. Simply turn off your phone or your WiFi and enjoy the day of freedom from uninterrupted thoughts this will bring. It is perfectly possible to make plans with friends in advance, organise your day, not see

the headlines and survive, thrive and relax with no phone. It is a great way to see how hassled and wired your phone makes you – something that is hard to see unless you detox for a while. It is likely you will see you don't miss out on anything and in fact have more quality time for what makes you feel good.

3. **Make certain times, activities and places in your life phone-free zones** I would start this with all mealtimes, whether at work, home or out. Commit to removing connectivity from other places and activities too: the gym, the supermarket, the car and maybe even your journey to work if you can. Again, we are creating boundaries of phone time and no-phone time. This is incredibly important with relationships: try committing to having your phone switched off always when you are with your children, your partner or your best friend to nurture and protect these relationships.

4. **Buy an alarm clock and a watch** Part of the problem and the recurrent impetus to look at the phone is when we use it as a clock, so it is being picked up all the time and you get sucked into the latest update or message. Likewise if the phone is your alarm clock by your bed, it is framing the start and the end of your day: it is the first thing you see when you wake up and the last thing at night. Even worse, some people will then also be tempted to look at their phones overnight when they can't sleep or they visit the bathroom. This fosters a terrible relationship with connectivity, a constant drive to be switched on, and empowers all that negative stress that is coming from the phone. Charge your phone away from your bed and replace it on your bedside table with a normal alarm clock.

5. **Consider coming off social media** The reason I would suggest this is because so many people have now told me that they have done this and feel so much better for it. Obviously it can be necessary for work or to connect with family and friends abroad perhaps, so try to reduce it to start with if that applies to you. But if you can, for now, disable an account or delete an app. Just try it and see how you feel for a week: you will see if you miss it, if you miss any social or necessary plans and if you feel better. It is hard to see the negative and detrimental effects it can have on mood until you realise how much better you could feel without it. Most people I know who tried this have not gone back to using it because the beneficial effects on their happiness have been so noticeable. It is a worthwhile step to try if you are suffering with any mental health condition or for anyone who needs a boost to their mood.

Scheduling

Having a timetable for a week and specifically scheduling your time is *not* about filling up your calendar, but actually about making the *right* time for the *right* things.

When you are feeling ill, mentally run down and physically at a low point, it is easy to let time pass by without doing the things that are protective and therapeutic for you. Illness can come with a lack of motivation, a lack of energy and a lack of focus, and you have to be focused on making time in the week for the activities that will be good for you. It doesn't need more than a few minutes to plan the essential aspects of your timetable so that they don't get overlooked. We are simply looking to flag up the important stuff that, right now, is a fundamental part of your recovery.

Timetabling and scheduling shouldn't be confused with trying to do more, and cram more into your already hectic and stressful diary. We are trying to take weight off your shoulders, not add to it. Scheduling and time management are actually concerned with making sure you give yourself time to relax, restore and rest – often those aspects of your life that you have let slip while work and illness have become all-consuming. You need to prioritise relaxing and enjoyable activities as much as the essential, stressful ones, and it is a good idea to schedule these in to ensure that happens.

A healthy week (and a healthy day) needs to incorporate balance and variety: Monday to Friday shouldn't look like a never-ending stretch of work with no break. Similarly though, you don't want to schedule in things that will be tiring or add to your stress. There is a balance to be struck within a week, where there are just enough breaks and variety for it to be manageable but not boring. For example, it would be unmanageable to try to exercise three times a week if you haven't done so before, and it would be boring to plan early nights too often. But a variety through the week, where each evening looks different from the last, can help see you through a difficult week at work by offering distraction, relaxation and joy. Balancing stressful days with more relaxed evenings where you know you will call a friend or relax with family helps to build your resilience and ability to cope. Variety is often cited by people as a protective factor in maintaining a good work–life balance, and this is something worth aiming for.

Each week spend a few minutes planning with a diary how the week ahead will look. Establish what you need to do and what you want to do, and schedule them in specific places. Look for variety and be realistic about what you can and what you will be able to do. Set yourself achievable goals: you don't want your diary to become a source of stress and failure. I even think you should go so far as planning when you are going to have early nights, have a relaxing treat at home, read your favourite book or phone friends. While they may seem trivial, these are parts of the week that are building up your resilience and maintaining or improving your mental state. But it is so easy to forego them when work, illness and tiredness get in the way. A little bit of scheduling will ensure these important things happen.

Plan a treat, however small or large that may look, and attempt at least one treat each week. I have one patient who told me she does this, where the treats range from lighting a scented candle or watching an old favourite film to booking a holiday. Psychologically, anything you do that is framed as a treat and feels like it to you will boost your mood and self-worth as you are nurturing and concentrating on yourself.

Lists and lists of things you want to do or should be doing are not hugely helpful for time management purposes, or your mental state. They are particularly unhelpful if you are stressed, as they can be overwhelming and add to your feelings of burnout. It is very easy to say 'I want to exercise more' or 'I want to read that book' and not do them because time dwindles away without it happening. It is far more productive, and therefore effective for you, to actually schedule when these things will happen, rather than just adding them to a never-ending to-do list. So rather than saying to yourself, 'I'm going to try and go to the gym twice a week', actually put it in your diary for the exact days each week when it is most likely to happen. You are far more likely to do something if it is a scheduled appointment, as it won't be cancelled or ignored. Once this happens for a week or two you will have developed a routine.

Planning a week and choosing what you do with your time more actively gives you back control. Illness and job stress make you feel out of control, and that powerlessness is an additional negative part of the equation. By controlling and actively managing your time in a week, even with the most mundane activities, you are empowering yourself and taking back the reins. Feeling you never have the time to do things, because of your work or your symptoms, makes you feel guilty, disappointed and worthless. Making the time to do things because you have scheduled them in ensures you avoid those feelings, and instead fosters achievement, confidence and a level of control you can take into other, more significant situations.

You may not have control over what is happening at work, but you can have control elsewhere in your life.

I have illustrated here how simple steps, within quite mundane or banal aspects of your life, can help you to create your journey to good health. Diet, exercise and the lifestyle adaptations suggested are all well-recognised ways of fostering good health, physically and mentally. Undertaking these changes, along with accessing the more formal treatment you need, should allow you to continue working while improving your health and well-being. These are simple changes to make but with huge dividends: investing time and effort in each of these aspects of your life will form the foundation of your ongoing recovery.

CHAPTER 7

Taking Time Away From Work

Sometimes, the first time I see a patient with work-related ill health is when they come to ask for a sick note, wanting time away from their job and the source of their illness. In a book entitled *Is Your Job Making You Ill?* it may seem absurd for me to now say that stopping work would *not* be my advice. It is generally not the solution to the problem and may not improve things. Although as a less experienced GP I would have assumed sick leave to be the cure-all, in fact now I try to warn patients against it: my overriding opinion, from experience and the evidence available, is that taking time off work is generally *not* a good idea.

But there will be people who buy this book and turn straightaway to this chapter, seeing no other option viable other than taking time off. It is possible that you may have tried the earlier chapters to recovery but feel the solutions are not for you, or could not possibly work in your situation. Or, they may be working but you still feel the need for time off, as an additional part of your recovery. You may simply be at the end of your tether, having tried every other option that has been outlined.

If you are considering taking sick leave, it is essential for you now to weigh up the pros and cons of doing so for you, your job, your career and your personal circumstances. This is the aim of this chapter so that you can make that decision fully informed and fully aware of the other options, and potential pitfalls.

It is important to understand the disadvantages as well as the benefits of taking time off work sick, and work through the consequences and logistics before you consider it a reasonable option for yourself. We therefore need to explore the following aspects of sick leave:

- The downside of taking sick leave

- Alternative approaches to your job

- When sick leave is necessary

- The logistics of sick leave

- What to do when you are not working

The Downside of Sick Leave

In the simplest terms, worklessness is not actually good for your health. Now that may seem an odd statement, given we are talking about jobs causing people to be ill in the first place, but not working at all, even temporarily, has been shown in studies to be related to poor physical and mental health.

At the very minimum, work offers structure, routine, self-worth and the opportunity to socialise. Of course for many people it offers a great deal more too, not least an income, but we are considering the basic personal factors here. These are factors that foster good health and wellness universally.

Even in all the negative work situations we have discussed, stopping work removes the positive and protective factors as well as those negative ones.

The routine of a working week provides structure – something which is positive psychologically for all of us. It can be very isolating and directionless being off work, even if you are facing ill health, as you lose a great deal of social contact as well as purpose, fulfilment and the imperative self-esteem that comes from that. Being busy and active in all situations provides a distraction from symptoms such as pain, and some degree of perspective: unstructured days confer no distraction but instead allow you to empower and concentrate on your symptoms, perhaps even worsening them. Not working can also contribute to stress as you worry about income, formal proceedings and jeopardising your career.

It is hugely important and valuable to acknowledge ill health, as I have discussed earlier, and face up to your problems as an individual; there should be absolutely no shame in that. However, taking sick leave is a very tangible and visual step – effectively an open and shared acknowledgement of your illness – that may come with its own pitfalls. Taking sick leave brings your illness and circumstances into the public arena where you can face unwarranted – and unjustified – stigma, judgement and questions. You are formally taking on the 'sick role' and at that point become vulnerable to people's opinions of your capacity and capabilities.

Of course we should live in an age where these judgements do not occur, and there are laws and regulations to prevent this discrimination formally, but it still happens. And it may not just include the opinions of your current workplace and associates but also, going forward, those of future employers if gaps in your CV or your sickness record need to be explained. I would hope the fear of such judgement and stigma would not stop someone taking the time off they felt they needed, but we have to accept that some workplaces, fellow workers and certain career structures are cut-throat in their approach and unsympathetic, making this a genuine concern in reality.

The biggest problem I see with not working is the huge hurdle of returning to work and the risk you face of being off sick long term, leading to joblessness. After just a two-week break, that first journey back to work, and the psychological barrier of returning to what has been a bad situation, can be very tough. More than once, I have seen this resolve into no return to work whatsoever.

We know that the longer someone is off work, the harder it is for them to return to any type of employment. Once someone has been off work for four weeks, the likelihood of returning is much reduced; after a six-month absence, there is only a 50 per cent likelihood of someone making a successful return to work. Long-term joblessness is hugely detrimental, not only in terms of the adverse societal and socioeconomic effects but also in terms of physical and psychological health. There is even scientific evidence to suggest that if someone is off work long term it can affect their family's health as well: the consequences are far reaching.

It is far better to engage early on with adapting your life, as detailed in the previous chapter, or adapting your job to stay in work.

An Alternative Approach to Your Work

As well as your own lifestyle changes and improvements detailed in earlier chapters, an alternative to sick leave is to consider adapting your work. There has been a cultural shift in the UK recently in terms of our approach to work and health: no longer are just two options available – in work or on leave. We now consider a middle way of working but with reasonable changes in place. This is the case for all forms of illness whether job-related, physical, mental, short-term and long-term. It comes from the recognition that to be in work is better all round. Thankfully this is now a recognised approach which employers and employees are used to as being preferable to worklessness and the long-term risks that confers both to the employer and the employee.

With this approach, as well as managing your health condition through medical treatment and self-driven lifestyle changes you are fostering your recovery from within your workplace – this is another aspect of your treatment. Rather than negating work completely, as was previously the status quo, this is a far better all-round approach to recovery. You safeguard all those protective aspects of work while reducing the detrimental ones. It reduces the stigma you can face and avoids the unnecessary 'sick role'.

This cultural change has come about largely thanks to the introduction of the Statement of Fitness to Work in 2010, which replaced the old-style sick notes. The so-called 'fit note' written by your doctor can keep you in work but in circumstances so you feel supported and less at risk. Like a sick note, a fit note has to state what your health condition is and how long the changes will be necessary. Your doctor can outline specifically what changes he or she feels will be beneficial, and which could include workplace adaptations, reduced hours, changed duties or an alternative timetable.

Your doctor takes on board the functional limitations you have from your illness and how it can affect your work. It is then up to your employer to establish what the adaptations could be which would help, and whether it is feasible. Someone whose depression is exacerbated by dealing with angry customers on a helpline all day, for example, could be offered an alternative phoneline to man that is less stressful;

or if medication side-effects make you fatigued, your working hours could be reduced or moved around to match your more wakeful times of day. Fit note implementation can also involve improving support at work, which may have been lacking and causing your health issues. I have had very positive experiences of this in my practice: patients maintain the fulfilment and global benefits of working, while improving their health.

Adapting your work has to be done as a formal process involving your employer, occupational health and a statement from your GP. Your employer may not be able to meet the adaptations, and if this is the case, you will have to follow the procedures in terms of sick leave. If a doctor has written you a statement of fitness with adaptations that cannot be met, then effectively you have been declared unfit to work and you can use that statement to take sick leave.

Start to have these discussions early on with your employer, and engage with HR and occupational health services to source the best approach.

And if you have no employer . . .

People who work for themselves can still get ill from their job, particularly from huge workloads and poor work–life balance. If you are in this position and have no employer to offer you adaptations or changes to improve things, you are going to have to change things for yourself. This is a hard call for someone who is self-employed, when often hard work gets confused with overwork: remember that slightly adapting your work is far more preferable than continuing to put your health, and eventually income, at risk. Adapting work as a freelancer or someone self-employed can mean putting in place even quite trivial changes that can improve your schedule or hours and lessen the health impact from your work.

You can simply look at altering one aspect at the start: this will feel easy to achieve and not too worrisome. Remove one trivial task from your week, for example, which will reduce your workload even slightly; can you delegate or outsource this? Consider how you can change your routine or restructure your day to incorporate strict scheduled breaks (even short ones) and a change of scene that can be beneficial. One day a week can you commit to finishing work and turning off digital connectivity by 5 p.m., no matter what is happening?

Whatever your situation, adapting your work can be a viable and healthy approach to take.

When Sick Leave is Necessary

Sometimes, of course, sick leave is absolutely necessary to improve your health. In mental health situations or physical illness, prolonged rest and removal of the external detrimental environment may be the only way to foster a recovery.

When your workplace is making you ill and an illness has been diagnosed, sick leave can be a formal part of your healing, allowing you to initiate medication, therapy or simply recovery time and rest. Particularly for the mental health conditions, it may be absolutely essential to take away the stressors and causes, to reduce symptoms and allow some recovery. It can be vital in cases of exhaustion and fatigue, where burnout has arisen, to put on the breaks and shout Stop! Sometimes this is simply the only way to recover and prevent further deterioration. Doctors and employers should be open to this as an option. Sick leave allows the space and time you have not had before to rest, recover and get treatment, but it also gives you room to think and reflect, which can foster your longer-term recovery.

Sick leave, weighing up the disadvantages and benefits as outlined, should be something you are open to contemplating and discussing with those helping you. It may be vital for some individuals and in some circumstances, and no matter what your situation can always be considered along with other aspects of your treatment.

The Logistics of Sick Leave

Managing your sick leave formally is very important to maintain job security and reduce your own stress whilst initiating your recovery.

Utilise the expertise of those individuals and organisations highlighted in Chapter 5 to ensure you follow the correct procedures: this will at the very least involve your doctor and your employer as well as occupational health or your union. It is important to follow the due process, be as upfront and organised as you can be and fundamentally follow the rule-book. Ultimately, this is the way to protect yourself, your job and your ongoing ability to work in the future. Illness itself can be a time of uncertainty which can be detrimental to you, and so you want to remove any avoidable uncertainty or ambiguity in the context of your sick leave.

You need to establish how your workplace manages sickness and sick leave by finding out what the formal arrangements are in terms of a sickness policy and the correct procedure; it is likely that HR or your line manager can advise on this. A sickness policy may be in place which should ensure your illness is acknowledged fairly, and will probably include details of how you are obliged to report in and manage your sick leave. It is not actually a legal requirement of employers to have a formal sick leave policy and there may simply be a specific process to follow. The rights and requirements of sick leave are explained more fully in Chapter 8.

Sick notes and fit notes

Part of the formal process of taking sick leave (and being paid) is to have documented proof of your condition and the need for sick leave from your doctor: this can be a hospital doctor, consultant or your GP.

A doctor will not usually provide a statutory sick note for less than seven days of an illness. If you are taking time off for less than seven calendar days, you are entitled to take this leave with no note from your doctor. Your employer may ask you to fill out a self-certification form on your return.

A sick note should be provided for you if your leave is longer than seven calendar days. This is, interchangeably, called a sick note, a fit note or a med. 3 (med. 3s are no longer used but the terminology still exists). It is officially called a Statement of Fitness to Work. This proof from your doctor will have to state your diagnosis and how long you need to be off work for: you should hand in a copy to your employer and make sure you keep a copy for yourself (I would make a photocopy or two to keep on record in case of any issues). Within the first six months of an illness, the maximum length of time on the sick note can be three months only.

It is not uncommon for me to be asked about changing the details or diagnosis on a sick note, which is perfectly understandable as employees can be concerned about stigma, discrimination or even job loss when they are ill. A doctor cannot lie on the sick note and has to document the illness that warrants the leave. However, they are able to write a less precise diagnosis that confirms the need for time off but affords some degree of discretion to you. Your rights to medical confidentiality remain paramount, and you can work with your doctor to give the details that are the most accurate that you feel comfortable disclosing.

What to Do When You Are Not Working

If you have made the decision to take time off from your job, it is prudent to plan and utilise your sick leave wisely. When taking sick leave, whether formally or informally, the primary aim of that is to aid healing and foster recovery, and you have to ensure your time off allows and promotes that, no matter what your ill health looks like. Simply having 'a break' will not foster a recovery alone: the time off will most likely help but it is only part of the healing process.

Being away from work is not a panacea; it may be one part of a bigger solution. Using the time wisely and effectively will mean it is successful and brings about the right outcome, i.e. restoration and healing. It is a chance to recover of course, but also an opportunity to change and move forward in a more healthy and well state of mind and body. This is true whether you are having a few days off or a few weeks. The time should be used as part of the recuperation process but also to structure your ongoing good health and recovery while back at work.

When we visualise time off from work, we imagine feeling free, zoning out and emptying our minds of the daily pressures. That is hugely important, but I really think that time off needs to be structured to be most effective. A totally free, unplanned sick leave leaves you vulnerable to returning to work with no improvements going forward and no proper recovery implemented. Just a tiny amount of planning and thought is necessary, and consideration about the end-goal of the time off, to make yourself better.

One of the big pitfalls, as I have said, of taking time off work is not being able to face the hurdle of returning to work when your leave is over, and it is a situation I have seen in practice too often. It is important to prevent this by remembering and staying mindful that time off is not the solution. It is a starting point, with the solution being going back to work in better health.

1. Engage with the treatment you need

The whole purpose of sick leave is to allow recovery, whether you are suffering with a physical or mental health issue. Having removed the source of the problem, this is now the time to engage with health professionals, therapy and any treatment you need to adopt. You now have the time and space to do this. You also have a strong impetus, if your health situation has become severe enough to warrant leave.

Focus on the fact that you want to use this time to effect change in your health, and that has to start with adopting a treatment plan for your ill health. That could involve engaging in a course of treatment you haven't been able to before; starting therapy; accessing your GP or specialist for proper management of your condition; or exploring support groups, either face to face or online. It could simply involve passive rest and recovery away from your work as a source of illness, but even in that situation exploring self-help options will be valuable. Now is your chance and the appropriate moment to have investigations or hospital-based treatments you have perhaps postponed or not had the time for. It is worth working through the treatment options listed in Chapters 2 and 3, and giving yourself the opportunity to seek the help you need.

There is often not the time or headspace during a working week to think clearly about possible treatments, especially when work has been the source of the problem. Use this time off to initiate your treatment plan and start a recovery that may not have been possible before. Far too often I am told by patients that they don't have time to start therapy, or they don't have a schedule that allows them to attend group support or appointments during a working week. Having sick leave can be a chance to do that and implement much-needed treatment.

Plan how your treatment will progress when you do go back to work – this is really important in terms of working towards the goal of a healthy return to work. Can you start with a therapist who will then be able to see you in the evenings? Will it be realistic to have time off for appointments once working again? Can you shift to a support group nearer work rather than home, or online, so you can continue to access help once you are back in work?

2. Rest – sleep and active relaxation

There isn't really one illness or health complaint that will not benefit from rest. Rest is an essential component of sick leave, no matter what the reason for that leave or illness. Rest is restorative and healing, and is as important as medication, therapy and other treatments. It is particularly important for work-related ill health, which has often been caused by work-load, exhaustion and stress, and when rest can be elusive.

Consider rest in two forms: sleep and relaxation:

- Sleep is vital and you should use sick leave as a chance to improve your sleep quantity and quality, especially when you haven't been able to before. This involves not only securing the right numbers of hours' sleep to feel rested but also having good quality sleep. If this is a part of your health that has been suffering, take your time now to adopt better sleeping habits and improve your sleep routine, as set out in Chapters 3 and 6. If your sleep has not been adversely affected previously, having early nights and uninterrupted long nights of sleep are still a valid and effective part of your healing. The physical and mental gains from good sleep are tangible for all of us.

• Relaxation is also an important part of rest. Rest does not just come from sleep but from mentally and physically winding down as well. Taking the opportunity to see a friend, read or go for a walk may sound simple, but they are easy ways to foster mental and physical relaxation. As we saw in Chapter 6, active relaxation such as meditation, breathing exercises or yoga is valuable to healing and learning how to wind down, release pressure and promote rest within your day. It is particularly effective for those suffering burnout, and you can learn approaches that you can continue after your return to work.

3. Structure your day

When your job is making you ill, perhaps the last thing you want to think about during your sick leave is a timetable. That is absolutely understandable, but having some structure to your time on sick leave is a good idea.

Sick leave, even for a few days, can feel like a nebulous expanse of time, and while that may seem attractive when you are ill thanks to a crazy schedule, it may not be helpful to be left with no structure to your day. If you are used to a routine, even a damaging one, it can be hard to plunge yourself into no routine at all and have blank, empty days in front of you. This seems paradoxical as space is just what you need, but it is a common feeling and even occurs when busy people go on holiday and find themselves surprised to feel tense with nothing to do. You are used to routine and in many ways routines are a positive and even comforting factor for most people.

Strict timetabling is not at all necessary: just plan your days simply to include active relaxation as well as any treatment or therapy you need to undergo. Often unless you plan your relaxation it can fall by the wayside, so this can be the minimum of a schedule. Or timetabling can be as simple as making sure you have regular mealtimes or wake up each day at roughly the same time. This can make it easier for people to cope with extended time off and returning to work healthy.

You want to do everything you can to avoid feeling negative about time off or feeling pointless or aimless. Taking sick leave is for most of us a huge change from a hectic schedule, and you don't want that to affect your self-esteem or your mood.

4. Focus on going back and plan your return to work

This is absolutely key to a successful period of time off. The most concerning part of sick leave is not being able to contemplate going back and facing again a situation that has caused you illness. Of course psychologically it is understandable to feel this way, but it can build up to being such a hurdle that you are unable to face going back. I have seen this in my practice countless times.

From the outset of your sick leave have your return planned mentally and physically. Specify with your employer your return to work date and psychologically in your mind see this as the end point to your sick leave. It is not a good idea to block out thinking about returning to work or adopt a stance of 'I just don't want to think about it'. You need to think about it so that you work towards it, aiming for a healthy return to the workplace.

You need to regularly and actively imagine and visualise being back at work. This almost seems like an unnecessary and trite action, but I have seen so often the return date becoming a source of worry and stress, and you need to guard yourself against that and confront it from the start. It may seem a bit odd to think about returning to work when you need to be away from it, but the idea is to make that return less of a giant leap, which it can become after the perceived idyll of leave. Be very clear in your mind when your return date will be, and what it will look and feel like when you start back.

You want a realistic and positive plan in place for a successful and healthy return to work, and that may take some planning. Make sure you use your time off to establish whether or not going back to work needs to look different from before. As well as adopting positive lifestyle changes for yourself, such as those set out in Chapter 6, do you need to plan with your employer any adaptations or changes for your return to work? This may involve a return to work note (a fit note) from your doctor, or you might need to look at a 'return to work agreement' with occupational health and HR.

5. Keep in touch with your employer

At the outset of your leave establish what contact your employer expects from you and is entitled to. This is crucial going forward to maintain good relationships with your work, and shows a respect for due process and any systems in place. Rather than a complete radio silence with work, this minimal contact will ensure a continuing relationship with work and is another positive psychological step towards a healthy return to work.

You may be expected to keep in touch with the HR department regularly, or with occupational health, and it may be that you are obliged to attend meetings or follow-up appointments as part of the sickness policy. Out of respect for the policies that are in place within your workplace, ensure you are up to date and forthcoming with sick notes, and make sure they are submitted to the appropriate manager at the correct time.

6. Take time for reflection

With the time and headspace away from work, you have the perfect opportunity to reflect on your job-related ill health. This is very hard to do within a hectic and damaging working week, but easier with the clarity of time away for your own personal uninterrupted thoughts. Time off affords you some perspective on a situation that has been all-consuming, and having proper rest allows lucidity of mind to think through all the aspects thoroughly. You may not have had the chance to do this before in the whirlwind of work and illness, so take the chance to do so now.

Self-reflection is a very important psychological tool to implement change and foster a recovery: I think of it as a system of looking back to improve moving forward.

Having the chance to reflect on your working life and illness can mean you adopt different behaviours and patterns going forward, plan better strategies of coping and are less likely to get ill again. This is not about mulling over or reliving the trauma; rather, appraising in your own mind the situations that arose and the steps involved that were either protective or harmful. Being away from work allows you that bit more objectivity than you would have had otherwise, which is incredibly valuable. It is a very positive step towards your return to work being successful and healthy.

Look at what has happened as objectively as you can and learn from it, so your return to work is better. Ask yourself the following questions:

- What happened?

- What did I do?

- What would I do differently?

- What has been working well?

While you may be off sick because of a difficult relationship at work, for example, are there ways in which you dealt with the situation that you could change next time? Are there better coping mechanisms you can adopt in future – the boss may not change, but can you change the way you react, or foster other, more caring relationships at work, or even ways to actively relax in the evenings so that the relationship impacts on you less?

Is your poor work–life balance really an unavoidable situation or are there factors you can change, now you have the time to think about it? Often with the benefit of distance you can see solutions when you have the headspace to reflect properly. This will be of huge value going forward, even if you can implement only the smallest of changes.

Taking time off work is not an ideal scenario but it may be essential to your recovery. Using the time to heal and reflect can make it an asset to your health and a springboard to a better working life. If sick leave is the right step for you, following the steps outlined in this chapter will help you to structure and use the time well, making it a viable and worthwhile part of your journey.

CHAPTER 8

●

Your Employment Rights

Given the amount of stress and personal distress work-related illness causes, it is important to minimise unnecessary anxiety and worry about your future employment, career and ongoing income. This book is all about protecting you and your health, and part of that holistic approach is to protect your livelihood and your job.

Being thrust into an unknown situation of illness is difficult for anyone with any significant medical condition, but with work-related ill health there is the added stressor of needing to know where you stand legally and the minefield of employment rights, job security and the due processes involved. Even if you have been in your job for many years, most people have never had to explore their company's policies and procedures or familiarise themselves with employment law.

Having even the most basic understanding of employment rights can be very helpful when faced with work-related ill health. For many people in these circumstances, in-depth knowledge of the relevant law and regulations will not be necessary but it is still worth having some insight. Knowledge is always power, and empowerment is important in illness; it is also comforting to remove uncertainty from what is already a fraught situation.

There are many people able to support and advise you regarding your employment rights and duties, as detailed in Chapter 5.

All workers in the UK are entitled to work in an environment where risks to health and safety are controlled, and this is the responsibility of employers. Thankfully there are laws and regulations protecting workers and their rights in this country, and we are very fortunate. There are laws to safeguard employees and their health. Crucially, mental health conditions, work as a cause of ill health, and stress are all acknowledged as issues that need attention. This should put employees in the UK in an enviable position.

What follows serves as a brief introduction to various relevant pieces of legislation and requirements for employers and employees in the UK that may be helpful if your job is making you ill.

Stress at Work as a Health Risk

The law requires employers to assess the risk of developing stress-related illness arising from their employees' daily working life. This duty for employers falls under the Management of Health and Safety at Work Regulations 1999: an employer must assess all the health and safety risks to which employees are exposed at work, and stress is included as one of those risks. Employers also have the duty to take measures to control that risk because of the Health and Safety at Work etc. Act of 1974. These are legal obligations for employers, but how they are implemented is up to the individual employer. There are standards for workplaces set out by the Health and Safety Executive, but these standards are not legal requirements but merely guidance. The Health and Safety Executive can enforce action though, where employers have not undertaken suitable and sufficient risk assessment. This is unlikely to directly affect you as an individual, but it is important to realise for any discussions you may have with your employer that the onus is on them to minimise any risks to your health, including risks of stress.

Working Hours

Workload, overwork and shift work are recognised causes of ill health and there are strict laws and requirements in place to protect employees from the extremes of these.

There are legal requirements with regard to organising working hours and shifts and these are set out in the Working Time Regulations 1998. The obligations on an employer when organising shift work also fall under health and safety legislation; they are part of the management of health risks as outlined in the Health and Safety at Work etc. Act 1974 and the Management of Health and Safety at Work Regulations 1999 already mentioned. Specifically in reference to shift work, the health and safety responsibilities involve managing and reducing the risks of fatigue; this not only protects individuals but the wider public on whom their work impacts.

The basic rights set out in the Working Time Regulations govern all employment, but they are particularly relevant to anyone doing shift work. They include:

- A limit of an average of 48 hours a week which a worker can be required to work (though an individual can choose to work more)

- For a night worker, a limit of an average of 8 hours' work per 24-hour period
- All night workers have the right to receive free health assessments
- A right to 11 consecutive hours' rest between working days
- A right to a day off each week
- If the working day is longer than 6 hours, a right to a rest break
- Four weeks' paid leave a year

An employee can agree to work longer than a 48-hour working week but this would be on a signed written agreement; it cannot be forced on you as an employee and you cannot be disadvantaged or fairly dismissed for refusing to agree to this.

Workers are usually entitled to three types of break: rest breaks at work, daily rest and weekly rest. If you work more than 6 hours a day, workers have the right to one uninterrupted 20-minute rest break during the working day: this would usually be a tea or lunch break. (Incidentally, this doesn't have to be paid, that depends on your contract.) Daily rest means that you have 11 hours off between working days. Weekly rest means workers have the right to either an uninterrupted 24 hours off work per week, or an uninterrupted 48 hours off work per fortnight. As an addition to that, an employee should be given enough breaks to make sure their health and safety isn't at risk if their work is monotonous, for example work on a production line.

Someone is officially a night worker if they regularly work at least 3 hours between 11 p.m. and 6 a.m., or an alternative agreed night period set out in writing. As night-shift work is known to be associated with health risks, a free health assessment must be offered to anyone working nights on a regular basis. This will ask you about conditions that could be worsened by night work or could impair your ability to safely carry out night shifts. It would include assessment of specific issues such as:

- Diabetes

- Heart disease

- Gastrointestinal problems

- Sleep problems

- Chest conditions with night-time symptoms

- Conditions requiring timetabling of medication or meals

- Mental health conditions affected by night work

- Pregnancy

- Any background history of night work and health problems

This may take the form of a simple questionnaire but must be written by a healthcare professional. You do not have to accept an assessment but the idea is for employers to take into account that night work might increase your stress levels. They are obliged to offer you regular repeat assessments and offer suitable other work where possible if you are shown to have health problems related to night work. You cannot be discriminated against if you do not want to work nights.

Sick Leave

Everyone is entitled to take sick leave as part of a recovery process, no matter what the cause of the ill health. This is enshrined in legislation, but there are also duties on you as well as the employee which need to be followed.

The process of taking sick leave will fall under the terms of your employer's sickness policy, which will set out what you are to do if you cannot work due to your health. For example the policy should outline who you are to report to at work regarding your sickness, and the time frame in which to do this. You have to follow this time frame, or report your ill health within seven days, to ensure you are paid for your sick leave: not informing your employer on time can breach your own terms of employment as laid out in your contract, jeopardising your job. Aside from any legal position, I would always recommend the benefits of talking to your employer as early as possible to keep positive channels of communication open. You want to maintain a productive partnership between yourself and your employer, who ultimately can help you in your long-term recovery.

Of course one of the important reasons to report your illness to your employer is to secure sick pay which you may be entitled to, although this depends on your contract and the length of your service. As a GP I am constantly amazed how many people say they are not entitled to sick pay, and it is hard to establish if that is because of an unfavourable contract, low earnings or the job set-up. You only have to be given sick pay if you are an 'employee', so some people miss out by being contractors or working freelance, even if they are working regularly at the same place. This is surprisingly common. There is a minimum amount of sick pay – known as statutory sick pay – that you are legally entitled to, but many employers give far more generous amounts reflecting your usual wage – again this is all formally laid down in a sickness policy.

If you have been off sick for less than seven days your employer can ask you for a self-certificate form to explain why you have been off. After seven days you have to get a Statement of Fitness to Work from your doctor – often called sick notes or fit notes, as we have seen. If you are planning with your doctor a period of time off to recover, much like after an operation, your doctor will usually include the first seven days so the certificate covers your whole period of sickness. The same Statement of Fitness to Work form is used to recommend adjustments to your work, if you are not going to be off sick but need some adaptations, as discussed in Chapter 7.

After any sick leave you do not need a statement from your doctor to prove you are now fit to return to work, if you are going to be continuing in your unchanged role. In fact if you decide to return to work before your sick note ends, that is your choice and you can do that after discussion with your employer.

In an ideal setting, going back to work after a period of sickness should involve – at the minimum – a return-to-work chat or, more formally, a Return to Work Interview. Returning to work if you are going to need your duties or hours adapted needs to involve a consultation with your GP, as a Fitness to Work Statement needs to specify what adaptations your medical condition demands. The GP can also be contacted by the occupational health department at your workplace to establish and confirm specific help you need in relation to your health and your work. You have to give permission for your GP to share this information, as it is subject to the usual patient confidentiality you have with your doctor.

Although not a legal requirement, if you are returning to work after a period of sickness, a written Return to Work Agreement can be drawn up between you and your employer. This is known to help rehabilitation back into work and is beneficial to you and your employer. It allows you both to be clear on what you are able and not able to do, and removes any uncertainty or potential misunderstandings in terms of your capacity to return to work. The agreement can take into account information from your GP, occupational health specialist and even your union representative. Like the doctor's Fitness to Work Statement it could be a plan that includes:

- A phased return to work, building up hours or days over a set period of time

- Changed or lighter duties to start with, in keeping with your medical condition

- Logistics such as team or mentor support, start and finish times, training or updates you may need – also possible travel plans and working at home arrangements

- A specified time frame and review period

If you are going back to work with a long-term change or worsening of your physical or mental health, your employer should discuss with you 'reasonable adjustments' to your working environment, which should allow you to continue your job just with some modifications to the set up. This is similar to the Return to Work Agreement but is a long-term plan to allow you to carry on in your job with your reduced health, new diagnosis or disability. This is in line with Health and Safety obligations and it is the duty of every employer to consider any health issues that might affect an employee's ability to safely undertake their job. This should ensure that due thought is given to appropriate adjustments in activities, hours or shifts that would be relevant to your health. Your employer is required by law – under both Health and Safety law and the Equality Act – to consider this information as part of their duty of care to employees.

The Equality Act 2010 ensures that anyone with a health issue or disability is treated fairly at work: it means that employers are obliged to consider these adjustments. Obviously adjustments have to be reasonable and feasible, and they may not be possible in your role.

The Equality Act is usually discussed in terms of people with physical disabilities. However, disability is defined by the act as an impairment which would have a significant adverse and long-term effect on a person's ability to carry out normal day-to-day activities. That is something that applies to a huge range of physical and mental health conditions, as I have seen in my practice over the last few years. Public-sector organisations, where there are higher proportions of work-related ill health, may be covered by the Public Sector Equality Duty, which makes sure employers show 'due regard' to the promotion of equality – this would include those with disabilities who may be more prone to stress.

Your Personal Medical Information

In order for any return to work arrangements to be as effective as possible, it will be helpful for your work to be fully informed regarding your ill health and the effects on you. Generally employers do not have the personal medical information of an employee, but in this case it will be vital for your healthy and safe return to work.

These special circumstances are covered by the Access to Medical Reports Act 1988, which sets out the legal requirements. An employer cannot apply for a medical report from your GP or specialist without your consent. You are legally entitled to decline consent for your medical information to be shared, and you are also entitled to see any report before it is sent to your employer. Your employer has to let you know they are requesting a report and explain the reasons why, which should be to create a return to work plan and agreement only.

This is a common request for a GP, and we are often asked to share the reports with our patients before they are sent. There is usually a time frame for this and you need to arrange to see the report with your doctor. You then need to give further consent for it to be sent on.

You are allowed to ask the doctor to change any part of the report which you believe to be inaccurate or damaging. Of course health and treatment is a very private aspect of one's life and usually confined to the four walls of a doctor's room: we are not used to sharing such intimate details and it can feel very invasive. If the doctor disagrees regarding any changes, a written statement can be added to the report stating your own views.

As with a fit note or sick note, doctors have to be accurate and truthful, and write a report in accordance with your notes. After a reasonable discussion with a patient, if there are genuine concerns about stigmatisation or potentially damaging details you do not want included, a doctor will try to accommodate this: we are always working with your best interests in mind and to the strictest boundaries on confidentiality, and we do not want to produce a report that unnecessarily compromises you or your position.

If you have not consented to a medical report being issued and shared with your employer, you are then expecting them to formulate any return to work agreements on the basis of the minimal knowledge they already have of you. This can make it difficult to put in place appropriate adaptations, as they may not fully appreciate the limitations or extent of your ill health. They may make inaccurate assumptions of your health or underestimate what you need, and so you will not get the best plan. Doctors are very used to advocating for their patients, and in certain circumstances may be better advocates than you can be yourself; for this reason it is always worth considering the sharing of your medical information.

Your health issues should not become public information at work, as it is essential that your employer keeps your health information confidential; it has to be managed as sensitive personal data and falls under the remit of the Data Protection Act 1998. It is not something that is going to be shared around the office, and should only be disclosed to personnel who strictly need to know.

Bullying

As we saw in Chapter 1, interpersonal relationships at work are a significant cause of job-related ill health. Accusations of bullying are common for me to hear from patients worn down by colleagues or a boss. When you are in the thick of this distressing situation it can be tricky to understand objectively what is going on, and whether you are being treated unfairly and inappropriately. Words like 'bullying' and 'harassment' can be overused and misunderstood: it is important to understand the details.

Bullying is not actually against the law. Discrimination, however, is unlawful under the Equality Act 2010. Both bullying and discrimination are behaviours that make a person feel intimidated or offended. Both types of behaviour, of course, should not happen in a workplace because of the damaging effect on individuals and on the company: it is no surprise that they lead to poor staff morale and absence through ill health. Bullying at work can take many different forms, including treating someone unfairly, singling someone out for specific treatment, undermining the skills and performance of someone who is perfectly competent, or stopping someone from seeking promotion or further education and training opportunities. It can happen face to face, within correspondence or social media and online. Discrimination is treating someone differently due to specific reasons known as 'protected characteristics' – namely a person's gender, disability, race, sexual orientation or religious beliefs. A specific type of discrimination is harassment, which is when bullying occurs because of these protected characteristics. Harassment is against the law.

It is an employer's responsibility to ensure that bullying and discrimination do not happen in the workplace, and this principle would usually be set out within a policy dictating behaviour and strategies to prevent it. This would routinely be a commitment from management to ensure bullying and discrimination do not occur and will not be tolerated. It may set out the procedures for dealing with bullying and harassment within the workplace if it is found to have occurred, and that relies on their prompt investigation of any claims.

As bullying can be quite a personal issue, often just between two people with one's word against another's, it is really important to note down and document what is happening; this can enable reasonable and accurate discussions at work and help to find a workable solution. I would recommend reporting instances of alleged bullying early on to your line manager or HR department, so that things can be dealt with quickly before matters escalate. In an ideal situation bullying would be dealt with informally without the use of any policy or official disciplinary proceedings, which are distressing and inconvenient for everyone. Mediation can also be a solution, particularly when it is just your word against someone else's. It can be an appropriate time to involve your union representative as an external advisor.

If any workplace issue has not been dealt with through

more informal processes, your next step is to raise a grievance. This is a formal complaint that obliges your employer to investigate appropriately using fair process; unfortunately this does happen in relation to bullying and work relationships, but can also arise from workload issues or poor support as well. Beyond grievance procedures, the next step is an employment tribunal, where your issues are dealt with by an independent body that rules whether your treatment has been unfair.

I would hope that when dealing with a job that is making you ill, knowing your rights as an employee and relevant employment law will not be necessary. But it can be helpful to at least understand what you are entitled to and, sadly, it may become essential when dealing with an employer. You may never have read your terms of employment or the policies and protocols at work, but if you are looking to improve your working life and your health, you and your employer will have to comply with the legal and safety requirements outlined.

·

CHAPTER 9

Moving On

After going through any illness and recovery, your main focus now must be your future and how it will look. You need to ensure you have done everything you can to build a sustainable plan that will protect your health and well-being in the long term. You should feel able to work and not be worried about the effects on your health. This will be an ongoing journey. With proper treatment and the right help, ill health can be resolved or managed so you feel better and able to move forward, physically and mentally. This should be the aim no matter what your job or your illness, and it is realistic for everyone.

Moving on is an important process, enabling you to forge an ongoing long-term recovery and well future. It comes at some point after any illness or trauma: with job-related ill health it may come with recovered health, the decision to leave work, the decision to make some changes or simply with time and acceptance of the situation. It does not necessarily occur at a defined point and may not always be premeditated. It is more of a dynamic process, and for some will be more passive than active, but along with the initial acceptance and acknowledgement of illness it is an important part of your recovery to better health. It may be that very little has changed for you but you have instilled more protective measures into your life; for others it will be that the acceptance and acknowledgement of ill health – and your job as the source of those issues – allows you to move on; and for yet others, very significant work issues may not have been repairable, and moving on psychologically will come from moving on physically to a new job.

Without a doubt you should be in a better place with regard to your health and your work than at the outset with the initial steps of facing the problem. Whereas facing the problem can seem frightening, confusing and stigmatising, moving on should feel positive, empowering and even exciting. You have faced a significant drawback and are now stronger and in a better position. Whether you have made some small changes to your lifestyle or more dramatic ones, the situation should feel improved and it is now time to enjoy a healthier and happier working life.

Do not lose sight of the fact that this is a recovery that you chose, created and grew. That is a tremendous personal achievement and should outshine any notion of weakness you may have as a result of your illness. This has been your success.

Moving to health and wellness from job-related illness will involve the following processes:

- Reflection

- Building resilience

- Sustaining your recovery

- Rewriting your narrative

- Leaving your job (sometimes)

- Finding closure

Reflection

Reflection is an important part of learning and growing, and part of an ongoing and sustainable recovery is to look back objectively at what has happened so that you can implement change and build the future. It may be something you are already accustomed to doing in your work as it is often cited as an important tool in professional development; there are psychological studies showing that self-reflection allows people to improve professionally. But reflection is equally important in self-improvement and can help you make sustainable changes in your life. I see reflection as an opportunity to focus on and adopt successes and solutions you have found, and to treasure positive and protective strategies you may have developed. It also involves accepting what went wrong or what was detrimental so that you can avoid repeating them.

Moving into a recovery phase is a good opportunity to do this, with the renewed sense of optimism you should have that comes with a fresh start. You can take the opportunity not just to reflect about your work and your health, but on other areas of your life too. As adults we get stuck in ruts, following patterns that we tend to forge unwittingly and then afterwards rarely question. We all have a tendency to do what we have always done, simply because we have always done it. Reflection can be a chance to question those patterns and shake things up a bit: what makes you happy and what doesn't? What have you been meaning to do but haven't got round to? What would be your New Year resolutions if you made them now? In fact, can you make them now? Are there people you would rather see more regularly but don't? What do you wish you had the time for at weekends? Do you actually enjoy what you currently do at weekends, or have activities just become a habit? Are there relationships you have which are beneficial and you need to nurture, or are there relationships that are toxic and you need to avoid?

Ill health – especially work-related ill health – is an all-consuming and exhausting time in your life. As you start to move on, hopefully you have some time and space for reflection that you almost certainly didn't have before. If you have done something to improve how hectic or chaotic a working week feels, you should have some room for thinking time to nurture yourself – you certainly deserve it. You also now should have some distance and much-needed perspective.

The process of reflection can be as formal or as informal as you need, but it is very personal. It needs a bit of time (it might be an hour, it might be a great deal more) to give yourself the opportunity to learn and grow. It is not a mulling over or dwelling on the past, however; try to remove the emotions from the situation and visualise it as objectively as possible. The failures and mistakes of the past are merely a springboard to change, not justification for guilt, regret or sadness.

Generally, self-reflection focuses on your strengths and weaknesses, the skills and success you have, the solutions you have used and the disappointments or strategies you wouldn't try again. Specifically with regards to work-related ill health, I would reflect on:

- What happened at work – why did it cause me to get ill?

- Could it have been prevented either by me or by better processes and procedures?

- What were my reactions to that situation?

- Which behaviours were protective and helpful?

- Which behaviours were unhelpful or destructive?

- How can I change that in the future?

- What positive strategies have I already adopted that will continue my recovery?

- Is there anything I can do to prevent this happening again?

It is very possible that the work situation that occurred and the illness you sustained were entirely unavoidable. But it is important to look at even the smallest lifestyle changes or protective factors or relationships you have put in place. Essentially you want to be able to use different behaviours and patterns in the future, along with coping strategies that will make it less likely you will get ill again and more likely you will remain well and working.

Building Resilience

Now you are moving on after a job-related illness, you will have developed increased resilience. This is an asset you now want to grab with both hands, nurture and take into the future for your ongoing health and well-being.

Resilience is often wrongly cited as simply being able to cope. It is in fact far more than that: at the very least it is being able to cope, survive and thrive after a detrimental situation. It is the ability to bounce back from difficult experiences with strength to move on. It will come from having certain inner resources and skills to manage difficulties as well as good support. An essential part of resilience is flexibility and being open to change, whether that change is forced upon you or chosen, along with a willingness to ask for help. This has very much been the *raison d'être* of this book as a self-help guide: showing you that you can accept a situation, take control over some areas and ask for support, so you are able to survive and thrive after ill health.

Having resilience means you will not only cope with difficult circumstances, trauma or stress but you can adapt to them, learn from them and continue to be optimistic about the future. It does not mean you are negating or forgetting the upset and distress you have suffered; rather you are not being crushed by them, but can stand up and move on. It reminds me of the old adage *what doesn't kill you makes you stronger*: you can bounce back after significant troubles with a renewed and perhaps even greater strength.

Generating resilience within ourselves depends on many things. There are some factors contributing to resilience that we can't change: genetics, upbringing, formative childhood experiences and your inherent personality. This wrongly leads people to assume that resilience is therefore a characteristic you can't develop or nurture. This is not the case; there are factors that contribute to resilience that can be built and developed and so it is not a trait you either have or don't have. It is also important to realise it is a combination of dynamic things working together – thoughts, actions, learned strategies and behaviours – rather than one isolated area of your behaviour.

Specifically focusing on work-related ill health and the solutions suggested in this book illustrates how your personal resilience can grow:

• Adopting specific lifestyle changes and improvements
  can grow resilience, in particular weekly routines
  involving exercise and relaxation. Both of these give
  you a greater capacity to cope with stress and adversity.
  If your mind and body have an outlet, your ability to
  handle problems increases. We know the positive effects
  both these factors have on mental health and well-being

and how protective that can be. These actions develop your resilience and form an important aspect of it in daily life.

- The active thought processes of acceptance, reflection and creating your own narrative are all vital areas of nurturing resilience through specific thoughts. Resilience very much involves focusing on the positives rather than the negatives. At the outset you did this by acknowledging illness was not a failure on your part but something to be dealt with (you did that inadvertently when you picked up this book). Appreciating that your illness has been a setback to learn from and adapt, rather than something crippling or insurmountable is a sign of resilience: these are the thought processes that make up resilience and they will continue to be helpful as you face the future.

- Being resilient involves taking control. This is hard during illness as many people feel out of control and weakened by uncertainty and powerlessness. This is why adopting micro-changes and enjoying the micro-successes that arise from them are so important: it gives you back a level of control. When you can't control your illness or destructive situations at work, being able to take control in other – even trivial – areas of your life leads to you feeling empowered and grows your confidence. These attributes then feed back into your resilience to cope with the larger, destructive situations. It is all about building self-worth and self-reliance which may be broken by illness but repaired elsewhere. Your resilience will be strengthened if you can see for yourself that despite work or health 'going wrong', other areas of your life are 'going right'.

- I dedicated an entire chapter to considering the people who can help with job-related ill health, because relationships and interpersonal support are known to be such a significant component of resilience. There is good research evidence from psychological studies to illustrate that even in detrimental work-based situations, the effect on you personally will be lessened by having a good team round you giving you adequate support. It is easy to understand how this will increase your capacity to deal with problems and therefore foster your resilience. The same is true of your personal non-work relationships: any positive relationship that you invest in and nurture will improve your confidence and self-worth. I see this as a layer of armour protecting yourself and enabling you to deal with difficulties. This is not merely because your friends and supporters will have the answers to your troubles but rather because having the support makes you feel stronger within, helping you to develop your own solutions: that is resilience.

It is very powerful emotionally for you to realise you have resilience and have already demonstrated it in action. You have set up buffer zones within your lifestyle and support network to protect you in the future, which form that resilience. Your resilience will continue to grow now; you should feel strong and empowered in your recovery – you have the resources to survive and thrive.

Sustaining Your Recovery

I hear too often in general practice, 'I stopped taking the tablets because I felt better, but now I feel ill again.' If you have successfully put measures and solutions in place to ensure your job is no longer making you ill, then you have to make sure you maintain them. Your recovery is not a static, finite process but more of an ongoing, linear one that you need to continue to nurture for your own health. Some of the strategies you have adopted will be long-term or lifelong ones as ways of safeguarding your mental health whatever is going on around you.

Undertaking changes whether through work, your lifestyle or treatment are what have made you well again, and it is important you maintain those changes. It seems a simple thing to say – *keep doing what you are doing* essentially – but it is easy to let good new habits slip and become complacent. You do not want to be constantly mindful of your illness, far from it; but be mindful of the processes you have undergone and how productive and protective they were, and maintain them. It has been a very proactive recovery, with hard work on your part, and now the hard work of maintenance needs to continue.

You have established a fresh start for yourself and you want to make sure you can sustain that; this is similar to the maintenance part of a weight-loss diet – you don't want that weight to go back on after your efforts to lose it. You've done the hard work and faced the difficult emotional and physical challenges; you want to make sure you continue on the same path so you keep your physical and mental health strong going forward.

Self-help and self-improvement are huge undertakings and really a massive triumph if you have enabled yourself to have better health and a better working life. It is very easy to take a pill and get better: it is far harder to take on board responsibility for your own recovery and work hard to bring that to fruition. Do not lose sight of that achievement and how you helped yourself and changed your health. Keep going with those changes and thrive on them and the recovery you have built. As I have discussed, there is a lot of strength and self-worth from success and micro-success: you now have that success to create a positive future.

It may be important to maintain the therapeutic relation-ships that have helped your recovery. Whether that therapy has been face-to-face, in groups or online, or with your doctor, ensure you have a plan for the long term. Formal therapy can be finite with a certain number of sessions; you need to be mindful of what that will mean in practice and how you will feel about that once it is finished. Some types of therapy may offer a step-down programme or less frequent maintenance sessions, so you check in once a month, for example, or less often. If you are under treatment from your doctor for mental or physical health conditions, once you are in a recovery phase you can still continue to be reviewed every two or three months, to ensure they are keeping an eye on you. This is a pretty normal scenario after a period of ill health and you can stay under review for a year or two, as you and your doctor see fit. In certain situations, such as addiction for example, when you would be involved in a recovery programme, or if you are on long-term medication, accessing your support or healthcare regularly will be essential.

The lifestyle changes, the protective relationships, the therapeutic solutions and the positive protective factors at work all play a role in your recovery and need to be main-tained. You don't need to stop building on that now. If you have found active relaxation to be a useful part of your recovery, for example, look for more ways to incorporate that into your working week or working day. Perhaps exercise has been particularly helpful, or nurturing your social network has really boosted your resilience: continue to dedicate time to those protective factors. You can continue to set goals and achieve more so you benefit from the positive mental health that will bring.

Rewriting Your Narrative

I really believe in the importance of owning your own narrative about your health and what happens to you in life. I have seen in practice and personally that this can promote self-esteem, good mental health and morale. It is particularly important in a situation such as job-related illness which comes with stigma, poor self-esteem and a dent to confidence and pride. Now you are on the road to recovery you can own your personal story and keep that as positive as possible. You are writing your own script and you want that to be optimistic and affirmative going forward, even when you are looking back on events.

As we have discussed, being ill is a negative life situation, no matter what the circumstances. It is even more damaging with job-related ill health, where two important aspects of your life have taken a battering: work and health. It comes with taking on the 'sick role' in your professional and personal life and becomes a very tangible and overtly negative situation. There is no shame and should be no stigma attached to being ill; this whole book is about admitting you are sick or that work is a problem, accepting this without shame and acknowledging that it can happen to anyone. But it is, by its very nature, a predicament to be in that often comes with a detrimental label attached.

The negativity surrounding being ill is partly thanks to the negative language we use around it, which is born of necessity and the natural way to deal with it. But now, as you move forward in better health you have the opportunity to change that language and discuss the problem in a different and more optimistic way. This is a very easy way to create the positive mental attitude we know helps to forge recovery and reduce suffering across all sorts of illness and trauma.

You can write your own script about what has happened

and what is happening now as you are recovering. Rather than discussing the episode in terms of the stress, the symptoms and the trauma, make the story about the flip-side: the help, the new exercise regime and the solutions you found. Rather than the nightmare, the failure and the problem, talk about the opportunity, the success and the solutions. The story is unchanged but you are telling it differently. You no longer want to emphasise the negative aspects of what has happened, but rather to empower all the positive ones. Positivity breeds more positivity and that is a real way to gain strength emotionally. This is not about lying or deleting the past, or negating the suffering or the difficulties you experienced. Instead you are celebrating the other side of what you did, emphasising those positive factors because these are the attributes that are going to carry you forward.

'I was forced to find a new role because the other one was killing me.'

'I'm starting a different role, which is good as I wanted a new opportunity.'

Same story. Different words. You are not changing the story or fabricating facts, but it creates a positive atmosphere around you, your perception of yourself and others' perception of you, and that is only a good thing. It's a very simple change but one worth working on. I think conversations and discussions around your illness and work should all take this form, whether you are discussing it with colleagues, friends or even in the privacy of your own home. You definitely want discussions to take this positive form if you are sharing your story on social media.

Own the story and make it a positive one. Think of it as a bit of marketing for yourself or political spin, to affirm your own confidence, your self-esteem and success to yourself and not just to the outside world. Celebrate what you did well rather than bemoan what went wrong. It is important to reflect on what went wrong and learn and grow from that, but that doesn't need to be the everlasting story. The story from now on is about the success of your recovery.

Falling ill, in any form, is not a failure: it can happen to anyone. But falling ill, having to leave a job or change a role will be packaged in your mind and in those of others as just that. Changing the narrative around it packages it as a success: this happened, I changed something, I created the solution and now I am excited about the way forward. This is the power of positive thinking and positive mental attitude that I see time and time again in general practice from patients suffering the whole range of physical and mental health problems. To be clear, I do not think positive mental attitude alone can cure illness, but it improves the journey, the distress and the capacity we all have to cope.

In the beginning it can be hard to think positively and switch to the glass-half-full point of view; speaking positively is a far easier first step that will encourage you to think positively and take that into your future.

When my husband suddenly left his job it was a tense and traumatic time, of course. It was stressful for us both across all areas, financially and emotionally. The processes were taxing and painful, and he faced what everyone faces in those circumstances – a blow to his self-esteem, an uncertain future and anxiety about everything from the bills to his career. The whole jobless period lasted months over one very tense summer before he settled into a new job and all was well. The funny thing now is that whenever anyone mentions that summer, either something trivial that happened or even the job loss itself, my children talk about how cool it was because daddy was at home to make great dinners. That is their overriding memory of the time, and that is what they always bring up both at home and to other people. Now, of course, they were protected from the situation and unaware of the stress we faced at that time, so that is their story about their father's time off. But this spontaneous positive narrative inadvertently became the family narrative about that time and rubbed off on me and my husband – this has become the everlasting story that we all take forward. The 'remember-whens' which all families muse over focus on the positive story about good food, not the negatives, of which there were many. We have all carried this upbeat narrative, rather than: 'Oh gosh, wasn't it awful when daddy lost his job ... ' This was unintentional – just a happy by-product of children's priorities – but I have seen from this personal experience how positive it has been. It has changed the adults' viewpoint and attitude going forward: we are not weighed down by what happened and all the negative aspects, but actually buoyed up by one small, seemingly insignificant, positive one.

Leaving Your Job

Inevitably for some people, a solution to job-related illness will come from leaving your job. It is undoubtedly not the aim of this book to encourage this, and I would hope that the strategies set out here will protect most people from that outcome. It goes without saying that leaving your job will not be a magic cure for most people. It comes with the huge burdens of financial worries, career repercussions and the uncertainty of joblessness, which is a significant psychological drain. But I have certainly looked after people for whom that was the only solution to a difficult situation or ill health, even despite their own and their employers' efforts to avoid it.

If leaving your job, changing your place of work or even changing your career becomes the unavoidable outcome of job-related ill health, then you have to ensure you regard it, emotionally (as with all the other measures), as a positive step of recovery. Having to leave work through illness can feel like a disappointment and a failure, and will undoubtedly impact on self-esteem, mood and anxiety. While it can be a very positive step of recovery, it is also a very dramatic and public leap, so you have to be mindful of the stigma that can come with it and, once again, of empowering the sick role. If you are already feeling ill and therefore vulnerable, you want to ensure you protect yourself from the worsening mental health that may result.

In addition to being the significant step that leaving your job is, worklessness itself is not good for your health. Being in a job, whatever the circumstances, offers the protective factors of socialisation, routine, security and self-worth. Even if you have to heal yourself by taking the decision to leave, and it is an essential and advantageous step, you are still losing those other protective factors. Therefore, you need to make sure you are still helping yourself in the ways outlined in Chapter 6; improve your resilience and build your support network to improve and then sustain your health as much as you can.

Do not make the mistake of thinking that leaving your job and starting a new one will be the complete answer. You have to manage your own expectations of yourself and a new job, and with the benefit of the experience of work and illness you have had, be realistic. As we have seen, the reasons people become ill from their job are many and varied and include not only the detrimental situations we face from our work but also our personal issues as well – our lifestyles, our characteristics and our world around us. A new job will not automatically ameliorate all these aspects; leaving your job is not so much a miracle cure but part of a holistic recovery, with many other things to take on board as well. So it is really key to implement all the other protective measures to foster resilience in combination with leaving your work. Be mindful of the strategies and lifestyle changes suggested earlier, and put these in place along with a new job.

You need to ensure in your own narrative that your decision to leave is packaged as success and not failure. It is vital with such a big step to reflect, accept and learn from the experience: you want to take forward a positive mental attitude to ensure you secure your own health and a new job. While the overriding feeling will be: 'I had no choice but to leave my job', you need to focus on all the positive aspects and lessons that resulted, such as 'I took control' or 'I had time to recover' or 'I made a really constructive decision'. It is a very brave decision to leave the security of a job and the security of doing what you have always done: use that strength for your future well-being. Leaving work really is the ultimate fresh start, and initially may feel like a great relief. Utilise that positive emotion as a springboard to make other positive changes to your attitude and your lifestyle.

The psychological processes of reflection, acceptance and closure are crucial if you have taken the huge decision to leave your job, but ensure you give yourself the chance to heal and have treatment. That luxury of time is often not available once you start a new role, and you want to take the opportunity to seek the help you need, the treatment and the therapy. That needs to be your number one priority from the outset, with the second being to find a new, healthier role and lifestyle to go with it.

Finding Closure

With any trauma or difficulty people will often say you need to find 'closure' about the event and to help you move on from it. What is meant by closure is really feeling that the matter is resolved in your mind and you can let go mentally and physically. You can accept what has happened and have given it an ending. It does not necessarily mean a problem is completely solved but that the questions around it are resolved and psychologically you are moving forwards. Essentially you no longer feel you want to be or are weighed down by what has happened.

I have seen how important it is to find closure after illness or a health scare, and specifically in the case of work-related ill health. One of the difficulties with any illness that I see in clinic is uncertainty. Not knowing why you got ill, how long it will last, whether you will get ill again and many more questions. As humans we like answers and defined processes and we don't feel so comfortable with ambiguity and uncertainty. Uncertainty, unfortunately, is par for the course with illness because there aren't always defined answers, particularly to the question of why. Closure is an attempt to deal with that, and will involve either looking for some answer that you feel allows the matter to be resolved in your mind, or accepting that some questions are simply unanswerable, seeking closure that way.

In terms of your work-related ill health, I have seen closure come from an individual understanding of why and how the detrimental work situation occurred, or agreeing with an employer some changes at work; discussing your health and circumstances with an employer or therapist can bring about closure; even the simple personal process of reflection can allow it. It does not have to be a formal procedure but rather a personal process you feel you have undertaken as part of your drive to move on and heal. It can be as dynamic or static as it has to be but, fundamentally, you need closure to survive and thrive.

People cite closure as a vital aspect of any recovery, and certainly that is true if your job is making you ill. You may need some answers as to what went wrong and how that can be resolved, to heal yourself and, crucially, to prevent it happening again. Feeling you understand what happened and what the different contributing factors were gives closure for you to create a new path. It is not to be confused with the issues being solved: you may get closure but still be feeling unwell, or still be facing difficulties at work. The closure means, however, that you are in a better position to move on and work through the problems. Seeking that closure adds further to your strength for the future.

For some people, closure will not involve finding answers but just a shutting of the door and moving on with their lives. Particularly with cases I have dealt with where toxic colleagues or bullying bosses have been the issue, there have not been answers or solutions to find. In fact, mulling over and reliving the stories sometimes has not been helpful at all, but more detrimental to patients' mental health and acceptance. My patients in this situation have found closure, and therefore their strength to recover and move on, by accepting that what has happened has happened, and that is it. They accept the status quo and concentrate on working on their own solution for the future. Closure for them has simply been 'Enough is enough' and a decision to get on and survive – nothing more complicated than that lightbulb moment.

Acceptance in this situation does not mean lying down and accepting what is thrown at you and the detrimental effects that has. It means accepting what has happened, accepting that you are not in a position to change it, but that you are now in a position to move on and control the effect it has on you.

If you do not feel you have closure at this point then it is important to look for it. It can come from reflection and looking back yourself or with a friend about what has happened, and going through those questions of what went on and why. It may come if you have the chance to seek help from a doctor, therapist or occupational health specialist: discussing your situation or your illness in this objective setting may allow you to find closure over time, and see answers or a deeper understanding. Closure for some may simply just take time and the perspective that brings to see answers, understand things and, hopefully, accept them.

Closure and acceptance allow you to face the future with all the strategies and resilience mechanisms you should have now created. You can reflect on what you have been through as a lesson from which you grew strength, and be optimistic about your future working life and wellness that comes from that.

You have built your own recovery and made it work for you, your job and, ultimately, your health.

Resources

To advise and guide you further on your journey to health.

Statistics

The Labour Force Survey collects data annually on the employment circumstances of households in the UK, providing official figures for the Office for National Statistics (ONS) for the government. These ONS statistics help to shape and define policy, funding and employment opportunities. The latest figures for work-related ill health can be found here: www.hse.gov.uk/statistics

Mental Health

- Royal College of Psychiatrists mental health information for all: these are very clear and helpful leaflets on conditions, treatment and types of therapy that can help you:

  www.rcpsych.ac.uk/healthadvice.aspx

- The mental health charity Mind offers support and advice as well as mental health information and online communities:

  www.mind.org.uk

- Mindfulness and mindfulness-based stress reduction:

  www.bemindful.co.uk

- Big White Wall – a safe online community for people with mental health symptoms who are finding it hard to cope:

  www.bigwhitewall.com

- Elefriends – a supportive online community for you to talk about your feelings:

  www.elefriends.org.uk

- If you are looking for a therapist locally and want to make sure you access the right type of therapy, these websites can help your search:

  welldoing.org

  www.itsgoodtotalk.org.uk

- Beating the Blues is an NHS-recommended site for computerised cognitive behavioural therapy (CBT) which has been proven to help people suffering with mild and moderate depression. It enables you to access therapy from home on your computer:

  www.beatingtheblues.co.uk

- Recovery programmes for addiction:

  For all types of addiction: www.smartrecovery.org.uk

  Alcohol : www.alcoholics-anonymous.org.uk

Drugs: ukna.org/

Gambling: www.gamblersanonymous.org.uk

Physical Health

- NHS Choices offers excellent patient information on all health problems, as well as on how to find a doctor and other healthcare matters:

  www.NHS.uk

- The FODMAP diet for irritable bowel syndrome can be found in detail at:

  www.kcl.ac.uk/lsm/research/divisions/dns/projects/fod-maps/faq.aspx

- Full information on treatment and coping with high blood pressure:

  www.stroke.org.uk/what-stroke/are-you-risk-stroke/high-blood-pressure

- An excellent resource to help you understand your headaches can be found at:

  www.nationalmigrainecentre.org.uk/

Your Employment Rights

- The most up-to-date government guidance on sick leave, fit notes, self-certification and the Statement of Fitness For Work:

  www.gov.uk/taking-sick-leave

- The Health and Safety Executive is the national UK independent watchdog for work-related health, safety and illness:

  www.hse.gov.uk/

- Fit for Work is a UK government scheme to give you access to expert occupational health professionals via telephone (0800 032 6235) or their website. If you are on sick leave for more than four weeks, your GP or employer can refer you for a formal assessment and a Return to Work Plan:

  www.fitforwork.org

- Citizens Advice can offer you free, independent and confidential advice on all work-related matters, including the law, your rights and responsibilities. Their website is incredibly detailed and useful, providing much of the information you could need, and they can also offer to speak to you in person or on the phone:

  www.citizensadvice.org.uk

- ACAS, the Advisory, Conciliation and Arbitration Service, can help you as an employee with advice and information on all aspects of UK workplace relations and employment law. Their advice is free. They can also offer conciliation and resolution services if things go wrong between you and your employer:

  www.acas.org.uk

Index

importance of 144
problems with 67–73
and caffeine 71
and exercise 71
and napping 71
and pre-sleep activities 71
psychological effects of 68
and sleep clinic 72–3
and sleep hygiene 70
and timetabling your
sleep 72
treatment for 69
underlying issues
concerning 70
and relaxation, as part of rest
process 174–5 (*see also*
relaxation)
and sick leave 174–5
SMART 57
social media 150, 155–7 (*see
also* connectivity)
consider reducing or quitting
159
SSRIs 45, 52–3
Statement of Fitness to Work
167, 171, 187
stress 35–9
symptoms of 37–8
treatment for 38–9
antidepressants 39
at work 182–3 (*see also*
employment rights)
sustaining your recovery 202–4

T
time off work 163–79
adapting your work instead
166–9
downside of 164
logistics of 170–2
and sick notes and fit
notes 171–2
necessity of 169–70

for self-employed 168–9
what to do during 172–9
engaging with treatment
173–4
focusing on return to
work 176–7
and keeping in touch with
employer 177–8
rest, sleep, relaxation
174–5
structuring your day
175–6
time for reflection 178–9
timetabling, *see* scheduling

U
unions 70, 188, 192
as source of help 123–5

W
work-related conditions:
accepting the problem of 10
acknowledgement of 29–31
back pain 4–5
blood pressure 21, 25, 68,
73–6, 139, 142, 148,
154, 217
case study into 62–3
symptoms of 74–5
treatment for 75–6
causes of 13–31
bullying 3–5, 18, 191–3
emotionally draining jobs
26–8
poor work–life balance
20–3
relationships 14, 18–20
shift work 23–6
workload 14, 15–18
wrong place, time, job
28–9
chronic, worsening 86–8

Acknowledgements

This book is dedicated to my husband, Adam, who single-handedly provides the fun, food, love and protection that keep me well.

With thanks and never-ending love to my favourite daughter, Lottie, and my favourite son, Jude: we all know that motherhood is really my main job and my favourite one.

I have a very special group of good friends and family who make me laugh, cry with me and know when to be there at just the right time, no matter what life throws at us. You know who you are and your support means the world to me.

Huge thanks to ROAR Global, especially Rebecca, and the team at Little, Brown who made my idea for this book into a reality.

With ongoing thanks to the patients of Abbey Medical Centre who inspired me to write this book and every week make me glad I am a GP.

In loving memory of Matt,
a great guy and we will always
remember you.